Contributions to Economics

The series *Contributions to Economics* provides an outlet for innovative research in all areas of economics. Books published in the series are primarily monographs and multiple author works that present new research results on a clearly defined topic, but contributed volumes and conference proceedings are also considered. All books are published in print and ebook and disseminated and promoted globally. The series and the volumes published in it are indexed by Scopus and ISI (selected volumes).

Marina Ranga

Single Market 2.0

Harnessing the Innovation Power of the European Green Deal

Springer

Marina Ranga
University of Warsaw and University of Seville
Sevilla, Spain

ISSN 1431-1933 ISSN 2197-7178 (electronic)
Contributions to Economics
ISBN 978-3-031-83219-2 ISBN 978-3-031-83220-8 (eBook)
https://doi.org/10.1007/978-3-031-83220-8

This Springer imprint is published by the registered company Springer Nature Switzerland AG
The registered company address is: Gewerbestrasse 11, 6330 Cham, Switzerland

Preface

This book is the culmination of an exceptional journey that started in March 2023, when I was invited to join the first cohort (2023–2024) of the Fellowship Programme for Economic Advice of the European Commission's Directorate General for Internal Market, Industry, Entrepreneurship and SMEs (DG GROW). As one of the 10 Advisors (Fellows) in this prestigious group, I was honoured to contribute alongside distinguished scholars in economics and innovation to DG GROW's policy making and analysis, focusing on topics of high relevance to the EU Single Market from a combined perspective of industrial, competitiveness, and innovation policies.

My role specifically involved an analysis of the green transition's impact on innovative place-based partnerships carried out in various industrial sectors of the Single Market in the context of the European Green Deal. The main objective was to gain a better understanding of territorial effects driven by the investments made by the European Commission through various financial instruments to fuel the transition to the 'net-zero economy'. This topic was a joy for me, drawing on over 20 years of experience in analysing national and regional innovation systems, including my recent six years of intense work on smart specialisation and place-based transformative innovation for sustainable transitions at the European Commission's Joint Research Centre in Seville.

There was, however, a new piece in the puzzle that demanded special attention: the European Green Deal. It quickly became clear to me that this economic, social, financial, and political behemoth of our time, particularly influential in Europe, was a game changer for the innovation and regional development mechanisms I had previously studied, bearing vast implications that could possibly take years to fully grasp. Driven by the desire to learn more about the European Green Deal, I took a deep dive into its history and underlying factors, seeking answers to a plethora of questions: How did it come into existence? Why was it necessary if the EU already had a robust body of environmental policies that started in the 1970s and was gradually consolidated up to present? What specific drivers led to its creation and through which intricate channels did it gain the power to influence nearly every aspect of our lives? My findings related to these questions are summarised in *Part I 'The European Green Deal: origins, drivers, structure and novel features'* of this book, which traces the evolution of EU environmental policy from its early days during the EU's precursor, the European Economic Community, to the launch of the European Green Deal in December 2019. This part outlines the progressive integration of EU environmental objectives into a comprehensive regulatory body that includes treaties, strategies, action plans, policy initiatives, etc., which have evolved organically at various institutional levels since the 1970s and have gradually integrated sustainability within broader economic and social frameworks, acknowledging the interconnectedness of environmental, economic, and social goals. This part also describes the nexus of scientific, societal, policy, and political drivers that converged before December 2019, urging the adoption of the European Green Deal as a strategic and accelerated response to pressing climate challenges. Novel features, such as a higher-level holistic integration of environmental sustainability across all EU policies, ambitious legally binding targets, and unprecedented financial commitments, made it stand out relative to prior policies.

Part II 'Impact of the European Green Deal on the EU Single Market' proposes an original exploration of the Single Market from an 'innovation system' perspective, centred on the quintessential structural element of the Single Market—the industrial ecosystem. The Single Market is conceptualised as an innovation system with the specific structural and functional format described in the innovation systems theory. The industrial ecosystems, as Single Market components, are themselves a set of interconnected and mutually reinforcing sectoral and technological innovation systems that operate within the boundaries of the Single Market's countries and regions and at global level. Applying the analytical framework of the seven functions of an innovation system, important effects have been identified within each system function, driven by selected research and innovation projects funded through specific calls of Horizon 2020 and Horizon Europe aligned with the European Green Deal objectives. These significant transformations in the Single Market's knowledge, technology, and skills base offer a promising outlook for the future, paving the way to a 'Single Market 2.0'. However, more efforts are needed to reap full economic benefits, since, with few exceptions, the technologies developed in this context have low to medium market readiness levels. A thorough evaluation of their impact will necessitate additional time, data, and research. The long-term success of these technological developments also hinges on the capacity to overcome many other challenges, including high implementation costs, structural disparities among the Member States, social acceptance, and the ability to build stronger synergies between industrial, competitiveness, and innovation policies.

Our findings, which are insufficiently captured by the existing indicators, can be a valuable input to policymaking. They can contribute to improved policy coherence and stronger synergies between industrial, competitiveness, and innovation policies. In the EU's rapidly evolving technological landscape, an effective exploitation of these synergies is crucial and can become the 'North Star' guiding the Single Market's journey on its road to the future: the Innovation Road.

This book is intended as a source of information and inspiration for a broad audience: seasoned academics, students, policy analysts, practitioners, and anyone with a keen interest in the transformative power of innovation in the twin transition driven by the European Green Deal. I hope that my findings will inspire other researchers to explore the intersection of innovation, industrial and competitiveness policies and advance our understanding of their intricate effects.

Sevilla, Spain
August 2024

Marina Ranga

Acknowledgements

I express my sincere gratitude to DG GROW's Chief Economist Dr. Roman Arjona and his team—Josefina Monteagudo, Stefano Vannini, and Frank Vandermeeren—for their valuable support in the development of the initial study that laid the foundation for this book. This work was conducted during my tenure as a 2023–2024 Advisor (Fellow) in DG GROW's Programme for Economic Advice.

My heartfelt thanks also go to Professor Andrzej Jasinski, Emeritus Professor and former Head of the Department of Market Innovation and Logistics at the University of Warsaw's Faculty of Management, for his unwavering support and encouragement to complete this book—a task that often felt like mission impossible, given my time constraints.

Finally, I am deeply grateful to my family for their enduring patience and support during the long days and nights this book took to complete. Their company during the sweltering Andalusian summer and the joy we shared at seeing this work finally reach the publisher were invaluable.

Introduction

Five years after its December 2019 launch and amid intense negotiations for shaping the new European Commission after the June 2024 elections, the European Green Deal is at the centre of heated debates about its future. Introduced by the European Commission's President Ursula von der Leyen as 'Europe's man on the moon moment' and celebrated by many, the European Green Deal also attracted sharp criticism for its high economic, financial, and social price tag. To better understand the variety of opinions surrounding the European Green Deal, some facts and figures are examined in this section, illustrating both successes and challenges of its implementation to date. That sets the stage for the central issue examined in the book: the European Green Deal's impact on the EU's Single Market and the main determinants of this impact. The book structure is presented, highlighting the specific topics addressed by each chapter.

In December 2019, the European Commission adopted the European Green Deal as the European Union (EU)'s new growth strategy aimed to turn the Union into the first climate-neutral continent by 2050. Reminiscent of Franklin D. Roosevelt's First and Second New Deal programmes proposed to the American people in the 1930s to use federal government investment and policies to overcome the problems of the Great Depression,[1] the European Green Deal mobilised unprecedented EU, national, and private funding for the ambitious goal of reducing net greenhouse gas emissions by at least 55% by 2030 compared to 1990 levels ('net-zero emissions'). To this end, far-reaching objectives have been set: providing clean, affordable, and secure energy; decoupling economic growth from resource consumption and moving

[1] https://www.loc.gov/classroom-materials/united-states-history-primary-source-timeline/great-depression-and-world-war-ii-1929-1945/franklin-delano-roosevelt-and-the-new-deal/

towards a circular economy; building and renovating in an energy-efficient way; promoting smart mobility; restoring ecosystems and biodiversity; and designing an environmentally friendly food system. A comprehensive regulatory framework strongly focused on sustainability has been designed and introduced in all EU policies (European Commission, 2019).

Introduced by the European Commission's President Ursula von der Leyen as *'Europe's man on the moon moment'* (Hutchinson, 2019) and celebrated by many, as e.g. *'a powerful beacon of hope in a world of confusion and instability'* (Sachs, 2019) or '*a paradigm shift of practical consequence for European—and via an example-setting effect—global sustainability policies*' (Schunz, 2022), the European Green Deal set in motion changes in virtually every area of the EU's economy and society. The Single Market—the EU's unified and borderless economic area that guarantees the free movement of goods, capital, services, and people, known as the 'four freedoms'—has also been impacted by these ample dynamics, as the European Green Deal has been seen from the onset as a driver of deep transformations in this area. Transformations were envisioned to take place through creation of new markets, development and adoption of breakthrough clean technologies, a shift towards decarbonised economies and transformation of the energy systems, a rejuvenation of the industrial manufacturing base and new jobs for a newly skilled workforce. An overall EU budget of at least EUR 1 trillion (European Commission, 2020) matched by national public and private fundings was planned to finance projects focused on the green and digital transitions through various EU financial instruments (e.g. NextGenerationEU, the Multiannual Financial Framework 2021–2027, InvestEU, investments of the European Investment Bank, National Recovery Plans, Green Bonds, etc.)

At present, five years after the European Green Deal's launch and amid intense negotiations for shaping the new European Commission after the June 2024 elections, the European Green Deal's initial promise *'to transform the EU into a fair and prosperous society, with a modern, resource-efficient and competitive economy'* (European Commission, 2019) appears to warrant reconsideration. The recent outlook on the EU's long-term competitiveness beyond 2030 claims that *'The twin transitions anchored in the European Green Deal and the Digital Decade, spurs growth and the modernisation of the EU economy, opening up new business opportunities and helping gain a competitive advantage on the global markets'* (European Commission, 2023, p. 2). This may appear as an overly optimistic assessment, contrasting with the mounting evidence emerged in recent years of significant losses in EU competitiveness, productivity and global market shares, declining leadership and relevance in comparison with global peers, with many EU firms either closing down or being overtaken by global competitors.

Is the European Green Deal still a viable strategy for the EU? Is its growth-centred approach adequately supported by the EU's resources and capabilities, or is 'degrowth' indeed '*…a purposeful strategy to stabilise economies and achieve social and ecological goals*' (Hickel et al., 2019) as many academics, youth activists, and policymakers across the continent that embraced the concept seem to believe (e.g. Kallis, 2011; Schmelzer et al., 2022; Stevens, 2023; Mauger, 2023)? Will the

European Commission in Ursula Von der Leyen's second mandate address the numerous critiques brought to the European Green Deal, including the fact that it has been overly politicised, insufficiently inclusive, and not adequately focused on regional and sector-specific needs (Bonfanti & Chiocchetti, 2024)?

In today's complex social, economic, and political landscape, a close look at the fine details is essential to better understand how the European Green Deal has performed so far and the variety of opinions surrounding it. For a balanced perspective, let's explore some facts and figures that reflect both successes and challenges of the European Green Deal's implementation to date.

a. *The European Green Deal at work*

The inclusion of the European Green Deal's 'net-zero' targets and policies in the EU Member States' 2021–2030 National Energy and Climate Plans and national long-term strategies[2] (e.g. reducing greenhouse gas emissions, increasing renewable energy usage, energy efficiency and building renovation, sustainable transport and mobility, better use of agricultural land, etc.) facilitated their rapid expansion. Some of the more environmentally minded Member States, such as Germany, the Netherlands and the Scandinavian countries, enacted some of the most ambitious environmental legislation in the world, often exceeding EU targets. For instance, in 2021 Germany brought the climate neutrality target forward to 2045, five years ahead of the 2050 deadline, and increased its 2030 greenhouse gas emissions reduction target from 55% to 65% (compared to 1990 levels), in an ambitious move to become a global leader in climate protection and production of climate-friendly technologies (Prognos, Öko-Institut, Wuppertal Institut, 2021). One year later, in 2022, the German government adopted the so-called 'EEG-Easter Package'—an ambitious package of reforms of the Renewable Energy Act (EEG), the offshore wind law, the energy industry law and legislation to speed up power transmission grid development- providing the regulatory framework for boosting the share of renewables to 80% of the country's gross electricity consumption by 2030 (Ivanova, 2022).

Sweden targeted 2045 too, introducing in its *Swedish Climate Act*[3] measures to reduce domestic emissions by at least 85% compared to 1990 levels and to cut emissions from domestic transport by at least 70% compared to 2010 levels. France's *Climate and Resilience Law*[4] adopted in 2021 introduced measures to accelerate the 'greening' of business and consumer behaviour, such as a ban on domestic flights where train alternatives exist, the obligation for cities or metropolitan areas of more than 150,000 inhabitants to establish a low-emission mobility zone before the end of 2024, and a new regional road ecotax from 2024.

---

[2] https://commission.europa.eu/energy-climate-change-environment/implementation-eu-countries/energy-and-climate-governance-and-reporting/national-long-term-strategies_en

[3] https://www.government.se/articles/2021/03/swedens-climate-policy-framework/

[4] https://climate-laws.org/document/law-no-2021-1104-on-the-fight-on-climate-change-and-resil ience_6f7e

In the private sector, companies in various industries adopted more sustainable practices, increased investment in green technologies and the circular economy, and aligned their operations with the EU's climate goals. The International Energy Agency (IEA) estimated that the global market for key mass-manufactured clean energy technologies will triple, reaching approximately EUR 600 billion by 2030, while clean energy manufacturing jobs will more than double from 6 million to nearly 14 million by 2030, if countries worldwide fully implement their announced energy and climate pledges (IEA, 2023). A majority of 57% of 500+ companies operating in high-emission sectors across 25 European countries committed to achieving net-zero emissions by or before 2050 (Agarwal & Sharma, 2023). In 2021, 43% of EU firms had already invested to reduce the impact of extreme weather events and to cut carbon emissions, and 47% of firms planned to make such investments in the next three years (European Commission, 2022, p. 32). Increasing investments in digitalisation have also been reported in EU firms, with planned investments in the long term for that purpose (ibid. p. 31).

Many firms pledged to become carbon-neutral in the next decades. In the automotive sector, for instance, Volkswagen Group's '*Way to Zero*' strategy[5] aims for carbon neutrality by 2050 and a 40% reduction in carbon emissions per vehicle by 2030. Volkswagen also collaborates with other carmakers, including BMW, Ford, Hyundai, Mercedes Benz, Audi, and Porsche, to produce Ionity, an ultra-fast, high-power charging network for electric vehicles in Europe along highways in 24 European countries.[6] Volvo Cars committed to becoming a fully electric car brand by 2030, phasing out internal combustion engine models.[7] In the energy sector, Shell's *Sky Scenario*[8] envisioned a pathway for achieving net-zero emissions by 2050 by transforming the global energy system through substantial R&D investment in renewable energy sources, carbon capture and storage, and hydrogen fuel technologies. In the aviation sector, *Airbus ZEROe Programme*[9] develops the world's first zero-emission hydrogen-powered commercial aircraft by 2035 based on extensive R&D on hydrogen propulsion and hybrid-electric technologies. Siemens adopted the multi-sectoral *Smart Infrastructure programme*[10] that creates intelligent and adaptive systems for buildings and energy grids, by integrating various digital and physical technologies to optimise energy use and improve the quality of life in urban environments.

Many companies also took steps towards a circular economy, by encouraging recycling, reuse, and sustainable product design, adopting more environmentally friendly practices, eco-labels and certifications, better informing their consumers and

---

[5] https://www.volkswagen-newsroom.com/en/press-releases/way-to-zero-volkswagen-presents-roadmap-for-climate-neutral-mobility-7081

[6] https://ionity.eu/en/ionity/who-we-are

[7] https://www.media.volvocars.com/global/en-gb/media/pressreleases/277409

[8] https://www.fourleafdigital.shell.com/WebApps/SKY_assets/index.html

[9] https://www.airbus.com/en/innovation/energy-transition/hydrogen/zeroe

[10] https://www.siemens.com/global/en/company/about/businesses/smart-infrastructure.html

helping them make more informed choices. For instance, Philips set out to achieve a fully circular economy by 2025 by designing products for longer life and improved recyclability.[11] IKEA committed to becoming climate positive by 2030 through initiatives in sustainable materials and product circularity.[12] The 122 stories from nine countries across Europe that applied circular economy principles, showcased in the *Smart Circuit* project, exemplify success in the uptake of recycling, resource efficiency, and sustainable manufacturing processes.[13]

The 'greening' trend has been rapidly advancing also among SMEs and start-ups. Climate tech start-ups in Europe experienced accelerated growth, becoming Europe's fastest-growing sector after fintech, with an overall worth exceeding $100 billion in 2021, double its value from 2020 (Talis, 2022). European SMEs benefited from European Investment Bank grants and low-interest loans for sustainable projects that increased their employment, productivity, and chances for a successful exit (European Investment Bank, 2024). They also accessed various funding opportunities of Horizon 2020 and Horizon Europe—the EU's research and innovation programmes—to develop green technologies and solutions. In Horizon 2020, for instance, SMEs accounted for 42% of the organisations that received funding, and 22% of that funding went to SMEs in the *Leadership in Enabling and Industrial Technologies (LEIT)* and the *Societal Challenges* programmes (European Commission, 2024).

The high levels of investments in renewable energy increased the share of renewable energy sources in Europe (RES) to 21.8% in 2021 (European Environment Agency, 2023a). The expansion of renewable energy projects is estimated to create an additional 200,000 jobs by 2030 in the wind energy sector in the EU (Wind Europe, 2024, p. 12) and the solar energy predicts more than 1 million solar workers in the EU by 2025, with prospects for further increase by 2030 (Solar Power Europe, 2023). The shift to electric vehicles is seen as the main driver for job creation in the automotive sector, due to the shift in technology, increased software in the car and in the product mix, as well as to the battery manufacturing and charging infrastructure (Boston Consulting Group, 2021).

The adoption of the EU Taxonomy for Sustainable Activities (ETS)[14] in 2020 as part of the European Green Deal improved the harmonisation of environmental standards and regulations across the Single Market and facilitated cross-border trade and investment in green technologies by identifying economic activities that are environmentally sustainable. Recent evidence provided by the European Com-

---

[11] https://www.philips.co.uk/healthcare/services/sustainability

[12] https://www.inter.ikea.com/sitecore/content/nl/aboutikea/home/sustainability/value-chain-climate-footprint

[13] https://circulareconomy.europa.eu/platform/en/knowledge/smart-circuit-circular-economy-success-stories

[14] https://finance.ec.europa.eu/sustainable-finance/tools-and-standards/eu-taxonomy-sustainable-activities_en

mission[15] shows increasing alignment of companies with the Taxonomy: on average, around 20% of companies reported capital investments aligned with the Taxonomy, mostly in the utilities sector, particularly electricity providers (over 60%). Value wise, around 600 European companies reported such capital investments to the tune of EUR 191bn in 2023 and EUR 249bn by June 2024, with an expectation to grow further. Banks have also started to use the Taxonomy in their lending strategies and in their assessment of companies' investment plans.

Behavioural changes occurred also in society. There is a growing environmental culture among the citizens and a shift towards more sustainable lifestyles and consumption patterns. There has been a growing demand for sustainable and eco-friendly products, such as organic food, sustainable fashion, and green household products, especially among the younger generations (e.g., Stahl et al., 2021; Beeson, 2022; Petro, 2022; Reichheld et al., 2023; Deloitte, 2023). Education and information campaigns have been launched by governments and non-governmental organisations to educate citizens about climate change, sustainability, and the impact of their actions (United Nations Climate Change, 2019). The widespread media coverage of the European Green Deal and its related policies has been instrumental in keeping environmental issues at the forefront of public discourse, influencing societal attitudes and behaviour.

The circular economy concept has been embraced also by the citizens. Urban farms, gardens, local food production to reduce carbon footprint and enhance food security (Quaranta, Dorati & Pistocchi, 2021; Jansma et al., 2024), and renewable energy cooperatives, where citizens invest in and manage solar panels and wind turbines to produce their own clean energy, are representatives of this trend. Several municipalities, local leaders, and NGOs adopted the *Zero Waste Cities* label and adhered to the *Zero Waste Europe*[16] network supported by the EU LIFE Programme for stimulating waste reduction and recycling efforts. The EU's *Renovation Wave* initiative supports energy-efficient improvements and renovations for homeowners (e.g. better insulation, energy-efficient windows, solar panels, etc.) and installation of smart home technologies and appliances that optimise energy use. Citizen engagement has been manifesting also in participatory democracy initiatives, such as public consultations and community-led actions to combat climate change, and in various forms of civic action, such as environmental strikes and protests, demanding stronger climate action from governments and corporations.

b. *European Green Deal implementation challenges*

Over the five years since its launch, the European Green Deal has also raised significant economic, financial, and social challenges. Due to important differences in their economic, technological, infrastructure, and regulatory conditions, the EU Member States showed different degrees of readiness to implement 'green'

[15] https://finance.ec.europa.eu/sustainable-finance/tools-and-standards/eu-taxonomy-sustainable-activities/eu-taxonomys-uptake-ground_en#1

[16] https://zerowasteeurope.eu/the-movement/our-network/

measures. Some countries and regions appeared to be benefiting more from green investments and job creation than others, amplifying national and regional inequalities. For example, Germany's robust financial and technological resources for renewable energy and green technologies helped the country become a leader in wind energy capacity, electric vehicles, and energy-efficient buildings. The Netherlands' advanced infrastructure for renewable energy, (e.g. offshore wind farms, extensive electric vehicle charging network, and a well-developed grid) enabled an effective integration of renewable energy sources. Also, Denmark's progressive environmental policies and commitment to renewable energy and green innovation accelerated the development of high wind energy capacity and ambitious climate goals. Spain's geographical advantages facilitated the country's leadership in solar and wind energy, with substantial investments in renewable infrastructure being made in recent years, especially in the southern countryside.

The environmental drive is quite different in other countries, such as those of Central and Eastern Europe, often called 'environmental laggards' (Börzel, 2003; Knill et al., 2012), that dispose of lower financial resources to invest in green technologies and face traditional strong dependencies on fossil fuels. Subject to the specific economic, social, and political conditions of each country, they adopted different strategies for the transition to renewable energy sources. For example, Poland, which is one of the most carbon- and resource-intensive economies in the EU, with a continued reliance on coal as a source of cheap energy, delayed the deadline for closing all its coal mines to 2049 and slowed down the process to this effect (Krzysztoszek, 2022). Bulgaria took a similar approach and rolled back to 2038 the plans to decarbonise the country's energy sector after strong demonstrations in support of the coal industry, driven by fears over energy and job security (Euronews Green with Reuters, 2023). Slovakia decided to close its last coal mines much sooner—by the end of 2023—following government's plans to stop subsidies for domestic mining (Hudek, 2023) and Hungary decided to do that in 2025, five years earlier than previously planned (Beyond Fossil Fuels, 2021). Romania committed in its Recovery and Resilience Plan to phase out coal mining by 2032 at the latest[17] and has already closed most of its coal mines, creating significant imbalances in its energy supply that was already weakened by ageing infrastructure and lack of a modern grid. Croatia decided to phase out coal in energy production by 2033, if not earlier (Renewables Now, 2021). Overall, these countries are confronted with important job losses and economic disruption, especially in the regions dependent on the fossil fuels industries, with higher costs for consumers caused by the higher production costs, and important social tensions caused by the incapacity to pay these costs.

It has become increasingly evident that the European Green Deal implies high financial, economic, and social costs for the EU that have taken a toll on the EU's global competitiveness. Evidence on the EU's economic decline has been coming from many directions. A 2019 JRC report (Marchinski & Martinez Turegano, 2019)

[17] https://mfe.gov.ro/pnrr/

revealed that the EU was already on a declining trend in the period 2000–2014 before the adoption of the European Green Deal, with a drop from 26% share in the world's total manufacturing in 2000 to 21% in 2014, and from 38 million people in manufacturing jobs to 32 million in the same period. The loss of market shares and downturn of manufacturing competitiveness was especially notable in textiles and electronics, with pharmaceuticals as the only industry showing resilience under lower economic growth in the EU relative to the world (ibid.).

The decline accelerated in subsequent years, and many voices sounded the alarm bell. One of the most compelling voices, the European Round Table for Industry (ERT)—an association of CEOs and Chairs from around 60 of Europe's largest companies in the industrial and technological sector—has repeatedly signalled Europe's serious falling behind in global competitiveness in their annual benchmarking reports and position papers. For instance, the 2022 report highlights Europe's declining capacity to invest in infrastructure and future technologies in strategic areas, having lost 30% of global market share over the last two decades and being far behind the USA, China, and South Korea in digital infrastructure, with insufficient investments in energy infrastructure & renewables (European Round Table for Industry, 2022). The 2024 report provides additional insights into the declining trend of EU productivity and global market shares, pointing to the EU companies' loss of leadership in terms of revenues and loss of relevance in comparison with global peers, many of them being overtaken by global peers and competitors (European Round Table for Industry, 2024).

Data of Eurostat, the EU's statistical office, also reflect the declining economic trend. January 2024 Euroindicators highlight a fall in the EU industrial production in November 2023 by 5.8% overall compared with November 2022, with an 8.7% fall for capital goods, 8.4% for durable consumer goods, 5.6% for intermediate goods, and 3.8% for non-durable consumer goods, while production grew by 1.0% for energy (Eurostat, 2024). The situation continued to deteriorate in 2024. July 2024 data published by S&P Global and Hamburg Commercial Bank show a further decline of the purchasing managers index (PMI), a rough real-time proxy for activity in the Eurozone manufacturing sector, and further contraction of this sector both in Germany and in France, the two largest economies of the euro area: *'Provisional PMI® survey data signalled a near-stagnation of the eurozone private sector during July as the currency bloc's economic recovery continued to wane. New orders fell for the second month running and business confidence dropped to a six-month low, leading firm to halt a spell of hiring which began at the start of 2024. …The eurozone manufacturing sector was again a key source of weakness. Production was down markedly in July, and to the largest extent in the year-to-date. As such, a rise in services activity stopped the overall private sector from falling into contraction. That said, the expansion in the service sector was only modest and the weakest since March. The two largest euro area economies continued to underperform the wider region. Output in Germany decreased for the first time in four months, while France posted a third consecutive monthly reduction in business activity'*. (Hamburg Commercial Bank, 2024)

The situation was appreciated as 'very worrying' also by the European Trade Union Confederation: '*The lack of investment we are seeing today is already having dramatic implications for working communities. …Factories are closing, and jobs are being cut in the very sectors [energy-intensive sectors, such as the aluminium, fertiliser, and chemicals industries] that lifted Europe to where it is today'*. (Euractiv, 2024).

Echoing this opinion, in February 2024, 73 business leaders spanning 17 industrial sectors presented the *Antwerp Declaration for a European Industrial Deal*[18] to the European Commission President, Ursula von der Leyen, and Belgian Prime Minister, Alexander De Croo during the 6-month Belgian presidency of the Council of the European Union, calling for a European Industrial Deal to complement the EU Green Deal and safeguard quality jobs in Europe. The Declaration acknowledged that *'To meet climate neutrality by 2050 and the recently communicated 2040 target, Europe's electricity production will need to multiply, and industry investments will need to be a factor six higher than the previous decade. This enormous challenge comes just as both large companies and SMEs face the most severe economic downturn in a decade, demand is falling, production costs increase, and investments move to other regions. …Our companies face this challenge every day. Sites are being closed, production halted, people let go. Europe needs a business case, urgently'*.

At the time of completing this book, the precise details of the European Green Deal under Ursula von der Leyen's second term as President of the European Commission had not been defined. The Green Deal is expected to remain a cornerstone of Europe's growth strategy, despite concerns that an increase in the far-right representation in the European Parliament could potentially sideline climate policy. Green investments are planned to continue, fuelled by a Clean Industrial Deal that was announced to emerge in the first 100 days of the President's new mandate. It would include investment in clean energy infrastructure and technologies, simplification measures for business, and an Industrial Decarbonisation Accelerator Act to support energy-intensive sectors in the green transition. Also, a new European Competitiveness Fund was announced for investments in strategic technologies, including clean tech, as well as measures to keep innovative start-ups in Europe and to increase spending on research and innovation (Greenacre, 2024).

Against this background, this book seeks to advance our understanding of the European Green Deal, more broadly, and its impact on the EU's Single Market. To this end, the book is structured in two parts with complementary foci.

Part I lays the groundwork for our exploration by focusing on the origins, drivers, structure, and novel features of the European Green Deal. Its three chapters address several key questions: What were the EU's environmental policies prior to the adoption of the European Green Deal? Why were these policies insufficient or inadequate, and what other factors called for an overhaul of the EU climate policy

[18] https://antwerp-declaration.eu/

framework through the adoption of the Green Deal? What were the main novelties of the Green Deal and how was it received?

- *Chapter 1* traces the evolution of EU environmental policy from its early days during the EU's precursor, the European Economic Community, to the launch of the European Green Deal in December 2019. It outlines the progressive integration of EU environmental objectives into a comprehensive regulatory body that includes treaties, strategies, action plans, policy initiatives, etc. These documents demonstrate that the EU had already implemented a robust framework of environmental policies, principles, and activities well before the European Green Deal. These policies have evolved organically at various institutional levels since the 1970s and gradually integrated sustainability within broader economic and social frameworks, acknowledging the interconnectedness of environmental, economic, and social goals.
- *Chapter 2* reveals that the European Green Deal did not emerge solely from an organic evolution of the EU's environmental policies since the 1970s but was also a response to a nexus of scientific, societal, policy, and political drivers that converged before December 2019 and urged for a strategic and accelerated response to pressing climate challenges.
- *Chapter 3* delves into the structure of the European Green Deal, highlighting several novel features, such as a higher-level holistic integration of environmental sustainability across all EU policies, ambitious legally binding targets, and unprecedented financial commitments, including the Just Transition Mechanism aimed to support regions most affected by the transition. The chapter also explores the varied reception of the European Green Deal, ranging from praise for its visionary and ambitious approach to criticism over its perceived moderate proposals, protectionist tendencies, and uneven policy implementation.

Part II is centred on the impact on the European Green Deal on the Single Market and the main channels for exerting this impact. It starts with an overview of Single Market key features and its links with the European Green Deal, moving on to an exploration of these links across the 14 industrial ecosystems from an 'innovation system' perspective. This original approach highlights several types of dynamics insufficiently captured by the existing indicators and calls for stronger synergies between industrial, competitiveness, and innovation policies.

- *Chapter 4* explores the key features of the Single Market and its links with the European Green Deal, embedded in numerous strategies and regulatory initiatives that have operationalised the European Green Deal since its launch in December 2019, aiming for broad-ranging impacts. Evidence of the actual impact of these links is still relatively limited, but data available so far indicate notable effects in several areas. Research and innovation projects funded through selected calls of Horizon 2020 and Horizon Europe aligned with the European Green Deal objectives have generated many of these effects. This is not surprising, as innovation is widely recognised as an enabler of environmental sustainability, but the 'mutually reinforcing effects' between research and innovation and other

drivers of sustainable competitiveness, claimed in recent policy documents, are not well clarified.
- *Chapter 5* presents the analytical framework for an in-depth exploration of the EU Single Market from an 'innovation system' perspective, using the seven functions of an innovation system as an exploratory tool. The Single Market is conceptualised as an innovation system with the specific structural and functional format described in the innovation systems theory. The industrial ecosystems—the quintessential structural elements of the Single Market—are themselves a set of interconnected and mutually reinforcing sectoral and technological innovation systems that operate within the boundaries of the Single Market's countries and regions, and globally.
- *Chapter 6* applies the analytical framework of the seven innovation system functions, using indicators and activities selected from multiple sources that are observed across the 14 industrial ecosystems. The findings reveal an ample impact of the European Green Deal on the Single Market's industrial ecosystems. The uneven concentration of R&I projects and EU R&D funding for the green and digital transitions across the industrial ecosystems may create new imbalances at the level of the Single Market as a whole and may affect the economic performance and capacity to implement green and digital technologies in the longer run.
- *Chapter 7* brings the book to an end, concluding that the innovation components of the European Green Deal induced substantial transformations in the knowledge, technology, and skills base of the Single Market, paving the way to a 'Single Market 2.0'. These transformations offer a promising outlook for the future, but more efforts need to be made to reap full economic effects. With a few exceptions, most of the green and digital technologies developed in this context have low to medium market readiness levels and need more time and money to counteract the high costs of the green transition. A thorough evaluation of their impact will also necessitate additional observation time, data, and research. The long-term success of these changes also hinges on the capacity to overcome the high implementation costs, structural disparities among the Member States, social acceptance, and the capacity to build stronger synergies between industrial, competitiveness policies, and innovation policies.

This book provides a novel vision on the European Green Deal's impact on the Single Market from an 'innovation system' perspective, highlighting industrial ecosystems dynamics that are insufficiently captured by the existing indicators. This evidence can be a valuable input to policymaking and can contribute to improved policy coherence and a better articulation of synergies between industrial, competitiveness, and innovation policies. In the EU's rapidly evolving technological landscape, an effective exploitation of these synergies is crucial and can become the 'North Star' guiding the Single Market's journey on its road to the future: the Innovation Road.

References

Agarwal, A. & Sharma, S. (2023, May 16). *Net zero pledges in Europe*. https://insights.issgovernance.com/posts/net-zero-pledges-in-europe/

Beeson, M. (2022, March 16). *European consumers drive the sustainability demand*. Forrester. https://www.forrester.com/blogs/european-consumers-drive-the-sustainability-demand/

Beyond Fossil Fuels. (2021, March 3). *Hungary brings coal phase out forward by five years to 2025*. https://beyondfossilfuels.org/2021/03/03/79874/

Bonfanti, M. & Chiocchetti, I. (2024, February 6). *A vision for delivering the European Green Deal in the new EU policy cycle*. Heinrich Boll Stiftung Brussels. https://eu.boell.org/en/2024/02/06/european-green-deal-new-eu-policy-cycle

Börzel, T. (2003). *Environmental leaders and laggards in Europe. Why there is (not) a 'Southern problem'*. Routledge. https://doi.org/10.4324/9781315256290

Boston Consulting Group. (2021, June 2021). *E-mobility: A green boost for European automotive jobs?* https://www.platformelectromobility.eu/wp-content/uploads/2021/09/20210623-E-mobility_EU-Report_PRESS_vfinal.pdf

Deloitte. (2023). *The sustainable consumer*. https://www2.deloitte.com/uk/en/pages/consumer-business/articles/sustainable-consumer.html

Euractiv. (2024, January 16). *'Very worrying': Trade unions alarmed by EU's industrial collapse* (updated: January 17, 2024). https://www.euractiv.com/section/economy-jobs/news/very-worrying-trade-unions-alarmed-by-eus-industrial-collapse/

Euronews Green with Reuters. (2023, January 13). *Bulgaria rolls back plans to phase out coal amid fears over energy and job security*. Euronews. https://www.euronews.com/green/2023/01/13/bulgaria-rolls-back-plans-to-phase-out-coal-amid-fears-over-energy-and-job-security

European Commission. (2019). COM(2019) 640 final. *The European Green Deal*. https://eur-lex.europa.eu/legal-content/EN/TXT/?uri=COM%3A2019%3A640%3AFIN

European Commission. (2020, January 14). *Financing the green transition: The European Green deal investment plan and just transition mechanism*. Press Release. https://ec.europa.eu/commission/presscorner/detail/en/ip_20_17

European Commission. (2022). SWD(2022) 40 final Part ½. *Commission staff working document. Annual single market report 2022*. https://data.consilium.europa.eu/doc/document/ST-6499-2022-INIT/en/pdf

European Commission. (2023). COM(2023) 168 final. *Long-term competitiveness of the EU: looking beyond 2030*. https://commission.europa.eu/system/files/2023-03/Communication_Long-term-competitiveness.pdf

European Commission. (2024). SWD(2024) 29 final. *Ex-post evaluation of Horizon 2020, the EU framework programme for research and innovation*. https://eur-lex.europa.eu/legal-content/EN/TXT/?uri=SWD%3A2024%3A29%3AFIN&qid=1706528145182

European Environment Agency. (2023). Dashboard – Renewable energy in Europe 2023. https://www.eea.europa.eu/themes/energy/renewable-energy/renewable-energy-in-europe-dashboard.

European Investment Bank. (2024, June 26). *Small and mid-cap companies across EU bolstered by EIB Group financing, study says.* https://www.eib.org/en/press/all/2024-219-small-and-mid-cap-companies-across-eu-bolstered-by-eib-group-financing-study-says

European Round Table for Industry. (2022). *European competitiveness and industry benchmarking report 2022.* https://ert.eu/wp-content/uploads/2022/06/ERT-Benchmarking-Report-2022-LR.pdf

European Round Table for Industry. (2024). *Rebuilding Europe's business case, working against the clock. Competitiveness and industry benchmarking report 2024.* https://ert.eu/wp-content/uploads/2024/03/ERT-Competitiveness-and-Industry-Benchmarking-Report-2024.pdf

Eurostat. (2024). *Euroindicators. 008/2024–15 January 2024.* https://ec.europa.eu/eurostat/documents/2995521/18319935/4-15012024-AP-EN.pdf/99ef8c47-94d2-00b9-2b36-821dd95350ce

Greenacre, M. (2024, July 22). Von der Leyen commits to Green Deal, reassuring EU clean tech industry. *Science Business.* https://sciencebusiness.net/news/horizon-europe/von-der-leyen-commits-green-deal-reassuring-eu-clean-tech-industry

Hamburg Commercial Bank. (2024, July 24). *HCOB Flash Eurozone PMI. Eurozone economic recovery fades further in July.* https://www.pmi.spglobal.com/Public/Home/PressRelease/566793e1194e4d55a9b020fbd612ae4d

Hickel, J., Kallis, G., Jackson, T., O'Neill, D. W., Schor, J. B., Steinberger, J. K., Victor, P. A. & Ürge-Vorsatz, D. (2022, December 12). *Degrowth can work – here's how science can help*. Nature. https://www.nature.com/articles/d41586-022-04412-x

Hudek, M. (2023, January 4). *Last Slovak coal mines to close in 2023.* Global Politics. https://globalpolitics.info/eu/last-slovak-coal-mines-to-close-in-2023.html

Hutchinson, L (2019, December 11). *'Europe's man on the moon moment': Von der Leyen unveils EU Green Deal.* The Parliament Magazine. https://www.theparliamentmagazine.eu/news/article/europes-man-on-the-moon-moment-von-der-leyen-unveils-eu-green-deal

IEA. (2023). *Energy technology perspectives 2023.* IEA. https://www.iea.org/reports/energy-technology-perspectives-2023

Ivanova, A. (2022, April 7). *German govt approves plan for wind, solar push.* Renewables now. https://renewablesnow.com/news/german-govt-approves-plan-for-wind-solar-push-780099/

Jansma, J. E., Veen, E. J., & Müller, D. (2024). Beyond urban farm and community garden, a new typology of urban and peri-urban agriculture in Europe. *Urban Agriculture & Regional Food Systems.* (published online). https://doi.org/10.1002/uar2.20056

Kallis, G. (2011). In defence of degrowth. *Ecological Economics, 70*(5), 873–880. https://doi.org/10.1016/j.ecolecon.2010.12.007

Knill, C., Heichel, S., & Arndt, D. (2012). Really a front-runner, really a straggler? Of environmental leaders and laggards in the European Union and beyond — A quantitative policy perspective. *Energy Policy, 48*, 36–45. https://doi.org/10.1016/j.enpol.2012.04.043

Krzysztoszek, A. (2022, November 8). *Poland to slow coal phase-out process, maintain 2049 end-date.* Euractiv. https://www.euractiv.com/section/energy/news/poland-to-slow-coal-phase-out-process-maintain-2049-end-date/

Marschinski, R., & Martinez Turegano, D. (2019). *Reassessing the decline of EU manufacturing: A global value chain analysis, EUR 29999 EN.* Publications Office of the European Union. ISBN 978-92-76-11253-2, doi:10.2760/30611, JRC118905.

Mauger, R. (2023). Finding a needle in a haystack? Identifying degrowth-compatible provisions in EU energy law for a just transition to net-zero by 2050. *Journal of Energy & Natural Resources Law, 41*(2), 175–193. https://doi.org/10.1080/02646811.2023.2187549

Petro, G. (2022, March 11). *Consumers demand sustainable products and shopping formats.* Forbes. https://www.forbes.com/sites/gregpetro/2022/03/11/consumers-demand-sustainable-products-and-shopping-formats/

Prognos, Öko-Institut, Wuppertal Institut. (2021). Towards a climate-neutral Germany by 2045. How Germany can reach its climate targets before 2050. Executive summary conducted for Stiftung Klimaneutralität, Agora Energiewende and Agora Verkehrswende. https://www.agora-energiewende.org/fileadmin/Projekte/2021/2021_04_KNDE45/A-EW_213_KNDE2045_Summary_EN_WEB.pdf

Quaranta, E., Dorati, C., & Pistocchi, A. (2021). Water, energy and climate benefits of urban greening throughout Europe under different climatic scenarios. *Scientific Reports, 11*, 12163. https://doi.org/10.1038/s41598-021-88141-7

Reichheld, A., Peto, J. & Ritthaler, C. (2023, September 18). *Research: Consumers' sustainability demands are rising.* Harvard Business Review. https://hbr.org/2023/09/research-consumers-sustainability-demands-are-rising

Renewables Now. (2021). *Croatia to phase out coal by 2033.* https://renewablesnow.com/news/croatia-to-phase-out-coal-by-2033-pm-759743/

Sachs, J. D. (2019, December 13). *Europe's green deal.* Project Syndicate. https://www.project-syndicate.org/commentary/europe-green-deal-is-global-beacon-by-jeffrey-d-sachs-2019-12

Schmelzer, M., Vetter, A., & Vansintjan, A. (2022). *The future is degrowth.* Verso Books. ISBN: 9781839765841.

Schunz, S. (2022). The 'European green Deal' – A paradigm shift? Transformations in the European Union's sustainability meta-discourse. *Political Research Exchange, 4*(1). https://doi.org/10.1080/2474736X.2022.2085121), https://doi.org/10.1080/2474736X.2022.2085121)

Solar Power Europe. (2023). *EU solar jobs report 2023. Bridging the solar skills gap with quality and quantity.* https://www.solarpowereurope.org/insights/thematic-reports/eu-solar-jobs-report-2023-1

Stahl, F. F., Emberger-Klein, A., & Menrad, K. (2021). Consumer preferences in Germany for bio-based apparel with low and moderate prices, and the influence of specific factors in distinguishing between these groups, sec. Sustainable supply chain management. *Frontiers in Sustainability, 2*. https://doi.org/10.3389/frsus.2021.624913

Stevens, J. J. (2023). *The relentless growth of degrowth economics*. Foreign Policy. https://foreignpolicy.com/2023/12/17/degrowth-economics-europe-climate-policy/

Talis. (2022, April). *The rise of European climate tech.* https://dealroom.co/uploaded/2022/04/Dealroom-Talis-Climate-Tech-Europe-2022.pdf

United Nations Climate Change. (2019, July 8). *Governments agree to strengthen climate education, awareness and public engagement.* https://unfccc.int/news/governments-agree-to-strengthen-climate-education-awareness-and-public-engagement

Wind Europe. (2024). *Wind energy facts and figures.* https://windeurope.org/intelligence-platform/product/wind-energy-facts-and-figures/

Contents

List of Figures

List of Tables

List of Boxes

Part I
The European Green Deal: Origins, Drivers, Structure and Novel Features

Chapter 1
EU 'Green' Policies Prior to the European Green Deal

Abstract This chapter traces the evolution of EU environmental policy, from its roots in the early days of the EU's precursor, the European Economic Community, to the launch of the European Green Deal in December 2019. It outlines the progressive integration of environmental objectives into a comprehensive EU regulatory body that includes treaties, strategies, action plans, policy initiatives, etc. These documents that have shaped the EU's environmental governance demonstrate that the EU had built a robust framework of environmental policies, principles and activities well before the European Green Deal. These policies have evolved organically at various institutional levels since the 1970s and progressively integrated sustainability within broader economic and social frameworks, acknowledging the interconnectedness of environmental, economic and social goals.

The early days of environmental provisions can be traced back to the time of the EU precursor—the European Economic Community (EEC).[1] The Treaty of Rome, signed in 1957 by six countries (Belgium, France, Italy, Luxembourg, the Netherlands and West Germany) and entered into force on 1 January 1958, proposed the creation of a 'common market' among these countries for the circulation of goods, labour, services and capital with a progressive reduction of customs duties and the establishment of a customs union. It also introduced other important provisions, such as the creation of a Common Agriculture Policy, a Common Transport Policy and a European Social Fund, and established the European Commission. Provisions specifically addressing environmental concerns were not included in the Treaty, and the lack of a legal basis represented a major constraint for environmental policies (Hildebrand, 1992).

Environmental objectives have been gradually included in EU treaties and other regulatory documents in the following decades, as sustainable development and

[1] The EEC was renamed the European Community (EC) upon the entry into force of the Maastricht Treaty in 1993, to reflect a broader range of issues covered beyond economic policy. The EC existed until 2000, when the Treaty of Lisbon incorporated the EC's institutions into the EU's wider framework and provided that the EU would "replace and succeed the European Community" (Article 1).

M. Ranga, *Single Market 2.0*, Contributions to Economics,
https://doi.org/10.1007/978-3-031-83220-8_1

environmental protection gained recognition as EU primary values. An extensive array of environmental legislation has been established since the 1970s, creating what is considered now to be the most comprehensive and modern set of standards globally, known as the environmental *acquis*, that counts over 500 directives, regulations and decisions (European Environment Agency, 2020).

Environmental policy became increasingly intertwined with the European economic and political integration process, gradually expanding its sectoral scope and influence (Oberthür & von Homeyer, 2022). 'Green Europe' emerged as a powerful narrative, becoming a successful new myth of European integration and giving environmental policy a functional role with political value derived from its capacity to generate legitimacy and foster a sense of identity within EU politics (Lenschow & Sprungk, 2010). The idea of environmental policy integration gained prominence on both domestic and European politics agendas, aiming at integration of institutions, organisations and their bureaucracies, in a dual process of internal integration (within the environmental policy domain) and external integration (between environmental and non-environmental policies) (Biermann et al., 2009).

Four broad periods can be distinguished in this evolution of EU environmental politics and policy (Zito et al., 2019):

- *The first period (1967–1984): Establishment and early growth.* Governments across the political spectrum, both in Europe and the USA, began adopting environmental protection measures in response to a growing social movement framing the environment as a rising concern in advanced industrial states. In the EEC, this shift was motivated by the need to safeguard the common market from diverging national environmental laws, which could become trade barriers. The EEC started to develop binding environmental legislation, such as the Environmental Action Programmes (EAPs), with the First EAP (1973–1976) considered as the start of formal environmental policy at European level. From 1973 to 1984, the EEC focused on creating directives to harmonise member state laws, particularly targeting air and water pollution. Since the 1970s, European environmental policy has seen a remarkably dynamic evolution, from a by-product of economic integration into a full-blown, independent policy area, with ever more issues and higher high levels of protection (Deters, 2019).
- *The second period (1985–1999): Reconciling market and environmental policy impulses.* The Single European Act—the foundational act of the Single Market, ratified in 1986—marked a milestone in European integration, including environmental policy. It formally introduced environment policy into the EEC's legal framework, in the form of a new 'Environment Title' (Title VII), that aimed to preserve the environment quality, protect human health and ensure rational use of natural resources.[2] The concept of sustainable development, popularised by the

[2] https://www.europarl.europa.eu/factsheets/en/sheet/71/environment-policy-general-principles-and-basic-framework

Brundtland Commission,[3] integrated economic growth with environmental concerns and sought to reconcile environmental protection with market-based solutions. The EEC, renamed as the European Community (EC) in 1993, primarily relied on binding regulatory legislation. Subsequent treaties, including the Maastricht Treaty (1992) and the Amsterdam Treaty (1997), significantly expanded and strengthened the commitment to environmental policies and objectives.

- *The third period (1999–2008): Challenging 'normal' environmental governance.* After the adoption of the Euro in 1999 by 11 Member States, priority was given to economic stability and competitiveness, while environmental goals were scaled back. The EC, renamed the European Union (EU) in 2000, continued to assert its global environmental leadership and maintained its commitment to environmental protection in international for a, such as the Kyoto process, but the focus on national economic interests became more pronounced and the pace of new environmental legislation slowed. Efforts were made to streamline regulations, favouring flexible framework directives and non-legislative instruments based on shared responsibility. The Lisbon Process of 2000, which initially included sustainability goals, increasingly shifted to economic achievements over environmental concerns. The integration of new Member States from Central and Eastern Europe in 2004 and 2007 further diverted attention from environmental issues.
- *The fourth period (post-2008): The uncertain future.* Multiple events on the political, economic and financial stage in the 2000s put the EU's integration project to the test. The EU upheld its environmental policies but reduced regulatory burdens and moderated environmental ambitions. Several trends have been observed in this period, from ecological modernisation (Machin, 2019) to a proactive role of the European Commission in shaping climate policy (Rietig, 2019). The EU enlargement created opportunities for increasing environmental roles of the Member States (Wurzel et al., 2019) and of the local authorities (Domorenok, 2019), as well as a shift from centralised to decentralised enforcement by citizens and NGOs (Hofmann, 2019). The environmental provisions embedded in the EU treaties have been complemented by a broad range of EU strategies, directives, action plans, etc., including: the 2020 Climate and Energy Package (2008); Europe 2020: A strategy for smart, sustainable and inclusive growth (2010); the Renewable Energy Directive (2009), the Energy Efficiency Directive (2012); the 2030 Climate and Energy Framework (2014); the Circular Economy Action Plan (2015); etc.

[3] The Brundtland Commission, also known as the World Commission on Environment and Development (WCED), was active from 1984 to 1987 with the aim to support sustainable development. The commission published its results in the 1987 report entitled *Our common future* that became known as the *Brundtland Report*, after the Commission's chairwoman, Gro Harlem Brundtland, Norwegian Prime Minister. The report introduced the concept of 'sustainable development' and developed guiding principles for its implementation.

To better understand how the EU treaties and related strategies addressed environmental issues, we will closely examine some of the most relevant ones next.

1.1 The Environmental Action Programmes (EAPs)

Official EU environmental policies are considered to start in the 1970s, when the issue of greenhouse gases in the atmosphere and their effect on rising global temperatures gained visibility in the public arena (Hildebrand, 1992). The 1972 Paris Summit of leaders of then nine Member States of the European Economic Community (EEC), a follow-up to the United Nations Conference on the Human Environment in Stockholm earlier the same year, pleaded for introducing a common environmental policy to avoid the risk of trade barriers and competitive distortions in the common market caused by diverse national environmental standards. In a declaration on environmental and consumer policy that was adopted at this summit, the European Commission was asked to draw up an action programme for environmental protection. In response, the Environmental Action Programmes (EAPs) were established, where the EU sets agendas and identifies areas for targeted action (Selin & Van Deveer, 2015). From the First EAP (1973–1976) to the current Eighth EAP (2022–2030), these programmes have been a cornerstone of EU's environmental policy and action.

The EAPs have evolved significantly since inception to present, reflecting the changing priorities, scientific understanding, and political contexts of their time. The early EAPs (1970s–1980s) faced significant constraints. One major limitation was the absence of a legal basis for environmental protection in the EU treaties of that era, so that from 1973 to 1984, the EAPs focused on the development of legally binding acts (200 by 1985 according to Knill & Liefferink, 2007). The early EAPs took mainly an intergovernmental approach, centred on market creation and externality management, with the directive as the main regulatory instrument, that could be tailored to specific domestic legal and policy circumstances of the EU Member States. Another constraint was the rigid decision-making process, divided between the European Parliament, which could only issue non-binding opinions, and the European Council, where decisions required unanimous agreement through intergovernmental bargaining (Deters, 2019). Under these circumstances, the early EAPs focused mainly on: regulatory frameworks and standards for pollutants in view of legislative harmonisation of national environmental protection activities and standards across the EU; integration of environmental policies into other policy areas, such as agriculture, industry, and transport; and remediation measures for air, water, noise and chemical pollution with impact on public health. The early EAPs tended to be more reactive, addressing specific environmental issues as they arose, rather than proactive, and were often fragmented, dealing with individual environmental components (e.g., air, water) separately rather than holistically.

Later EAPs (1990s–present) took a more comprehensive approach, with more target sectors and themes and a stronger integration of environmental policies into all sectors, including energy, transport, agriculture, and industry. The Fifth EAP[4] (1993–2000) expanded its thematic area to seven environmental strategic areas (global warming, acidification, biodiversity, management of water resources, urban environment, coastal zones and waste management) and embraced sustainable development and better management of natural resources as core principles. The Sixth EAP[5] (2002–2012) reframed the EU environmental priorities around four themes and seven strategic areas[6] and made climate change a central goal, with specific targets for reducing greenhouse gas emissions and promoting renewable energy. However, an evaluation of the Sixth EAP concluded that many fields of environmental policy that have been on EAP agendas for several years were addressed inadequately or not at all, mainly due to the lack of will to take decisive action to putting knowledge, and sometimes even political decisions, into practice (European Economic and Social Committee, 2012).

The Seventh EAP[7] (2014–2020) introduced the vision of turning the EU into a resource-efficient, green, and competitive low-carbon economy up to 2020 and beyond to 2050, based on circular economy, biodiversity, and sustainable management of resources. This orientation was influenced by the European Commission's *Europe 2020: A strategy for smart, sustainable and inclusive growth* (European Commission, 2010) that included climate change and energy among the five 'headline targets' for 2020 and promoted seven flagship initiatives.[8] Among them, the 'Resource-efficient Europe' flagship was particularly influential, emphasising the importance of the transition to a low-carbon economy and resource efficiency. The Seventh EAP also underlined the role of innovation and technology in achieving environmental goals and promoted green technologies, eco-innovation, and research and development for environmental objectives and biodiversity. The concept of a circular economy, aimed to reduce waste and make the most of resources, became a key focus, reflecting a shift towards more sustainable production and consumption patterns. The Eighth EAP[9] (2022–2030) consolidated these objectives, reiterating the EU's long-term vision to 2050 and building on the Green Deal.

Later EAPs differed from the early ones by adopting a more proactive approach and incorporating principles such as the precautionary principle and the 'polluter

[4]https://eur-lex.europa.eu/legal-content/EN/TXT/HTML/?uri=LEGISSUM:l28062

[5]https://eur-lex.europa.eu/legal-content/EN/TXT/HTML/?uri=URISERV:l28027

[6]The Sixth EAP included four priority themes for European environmental policy: (1) tackling climate change, (2) protection of nature and biodiversity, (3) environment, health and quality of life, and (4) sustainable use and management of natural resources and wastes. Seven thematic strategies were declared in these priority themes: air pollution, the marine environment, waste prevention and recycling, sustainable use of natural resources, the urban environment, soil protection and sustainable use of pesticides.

[7]https://eur-lex.europa.eu/legal-content/EN/TXT/?uri=CELEX:32013D1386

[8]The six flagship initiatives included: Innovation Union; Youth on the Move; Digital Agenda for Europe; Resource-efficient Europe; An Industrial Policy for the Globalisation Era.

[9]https://eur-lex.europa.eu/EN/legal-content/summary/eu-environment-action-programme-to-2030.html

pays' principle, to prevent environmental problems rather than merely react to them. These programmes took a more holistic view of environmental protection, recognising the links between various environmental issues and the need for comprehensive solutions. Later EAPs also placed greater emphasis on stakeholder involvement in environmental decision-making processes, including governments, businesses, non-governmental organizations, and citizens, in view of improving environmental governance by enhancing transparency and accountability.

Another notable feature is the role that the EAPs, especially the early ones, had in building the EU's institutional capacity to manage environmental issues. At the level of the European Commission, after 15 years with no department dedicated to environmental issues, the Environmental Unit was created in 1973 within the Directorate-General Industry. In 1981 the Directorate General Environment (DG ENV) was established, with the mission to 'protect, preserve and improve the environment for present and future generations, proposing and implementing policies that ensure a high level of environmental protection and preserve the quality of life of EU citizens'.[10] After the Fifth EAP (1993–2000), DG ENV's policymaking adopted a more open and inclusive approach with a stronger involvement of social and economic partners.

Environmental institutions outside the EU were also established, mainly since the 1990s. Several key agencies and bodies responsible for environmental protection were set up to support the EAP implementation, offer scientific expertise to inform policymaking, monitor environmental conditions and collect data, to raise public awareness and ensure compliance with EU environmental legislation. Examples include the European Environment Agency (EEA), the European Chemicals Agency (ECHA), the European Food Safety Authority (EFSA) and the European Agency for Safety and Health at Work (EU-OSHA).[11] Also, the European Environmental Bureau (EEB) was established in 1974 as an umbrella organization for European environmental NGOs, advocating for stronger environmental policies and monitoring the implementation of EAPs. These agencies contributed to a comprehensive and coordinated approach to environmental protection in the EU and continue to advance the EU's environmental objectives, addressing new environmental challenges.

1.2 The Single European Act (SEA)

The Single European Act (SEA), signed in 1986 and coming into force in 1987, committed the EEC member countries to a timetable for economic integration. It set the objective of creating a single market within the EEC by 31 December 1992, a

[10] https://knowledge4policy.ec.europa.eu/organisation/dg-env-dg-environment_en

[11] The European Environment Agency (EEA) was established in 1990 and became operational in 1994, the European Chemicals Agency (ECHA) in 2007, the European Food Safety Authority (EFSA) in 2002, and the European Agency for Safety and Health at Work (EU-OSHA) in 1994

Table 1.1 Legislative output in environmental policy

Phase	Legislative acts	Duration (months)	Acts per month
1970—SEA	173	210	0.82
SEA—Enlargement	330	202	1.63
Enlargement—2018	232	176	1.32

Note: Directives, regulations and decisions adopted by the European Council in the area of environmental policy (Eur-Lex Directory Code 15.10)
1970: January 1, 1970. SEA: June 30, 1987. Enlargement: Eastern enlargement on May 1, 2004. 2018: December 31, 2018. Abbreviations: *EU* European Union, *SEA* Single European Act
Source: Deters (2019), p. 318

single European currency and unified foreign and domestic policies.[12] Driven by dissatisfaction over the lack of free trade among EEC members in the 1980s, the SEA aimed to harmonise laws across the EEC countries and eliminate non-tariff barriers to cross-border intra-community trade and investment. Besides its impact on the single market, the SEA also influenced the EEC's environmental policies by introducing the first legal basis for a common environmental policy through the new 'Environment Title' (Title VII). This provision aimed to preserve environment quality, protect human health and ensure rational use of natural resources.[13] Subsequent treaty revisions strengthened the EEC's commitment to environmental protection and the role of the European Parliament in its development (ibid.). The SEA included key environmental principles such as the precautionary principle, the 'polluter pays' principle and the principle of preventive action, which became fundamental to the community environmental legislation and policy development. The SEA also mandated the integration of environmental protection requirements into the definition and implementation of other community policies in various sectors, such as agriculture, transport, and industry, contributing thus to the emerging concept of sustainable development.

The legal basis provided by the first EAP and the SEA enabled the adoption of numerous directives on air quality, water quality, waste management and nature conservation and supported the development and implementation of the subsequent Environmental Action Programmes (EAPs), with a peak around the first EU enlargement around 2004 (Deters, 2019), as shown in Table 1.1. The EEC's legislative action increased overall after the SEA entered into force in July 1987, with the number of acts per month almost doubling between SEA and the Treaty of Maastricht in 1992 (Fig. 1.1). SEA's provisions encouraged the EEC to play a more active role in international environmental negotiations and agreements, positioning it as a leader in global environmental governance and climate change initiatives.

[12]https://eur-lex.europa.eu/legal-content/EN/TXT/PDF/?uri=CELEX:11986U/TXT

[13]https://www.europarl.europa.eu/factsheets/en/sheet/71/environment-policy-general-principles-and-basic-framework

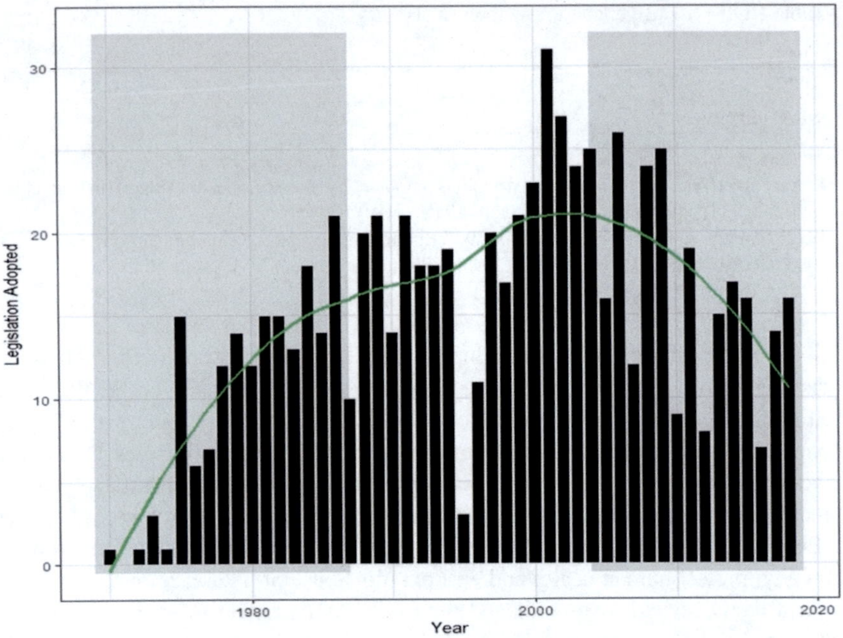

Fig. 1.1 Directives, regulations and decisions adopted by the Council and (where applicable) the European Parliament in the field of environment. Source: Deters (2019), p. 319

1.3 The Maastricht Treaty (Treaty on European Union)

A few years later, the Maastricht Treaty (also known as the Treaty on European Union), signed in 1992 and coming into force in 1993, included important new provisions for the EU's green policies.[14] It made the environment (Title XVI) an official policy area[15] and established the co-decision procedure, allowing the European Parliament and the Council to jointly decide on environmental legislation. It introduced the Qualified Majority Voting (QMV) in the European Council as the general rule for environmental issues, to streamline decision-making and facilitate consensus-building among Member States. This move enhanced democratic decision-making in environmental matters, increasing the powers of the European Parliament, while lessening the legislative influence of the European Commission,

[14] https://eur-lex.europa.eu/legal-content/EN/TXT/?uri=CELEX:11992M/TXT

[15] The Treaty's Article 130 provided a clear legal basis for environmental policies, by specifying key objectives such as a prudent and rational utilization of natural resources, use of the precautionary and preventive action principles, and the economic and social development of the Community as a whole and the balanced development of its regions.

which was left with a more informal agenda-setting influence (Tsebelis & Garrett, 2000).

The Maastricht Treaty emphasised the subsidiarity principle and urged Member States to assess their environmental impact and uphold the principle of sustainable growth.[16] By explicitly referring to environmental objectives, such as sustainable development, respect for the environment and a high quality of the environment, the Maastricht Treaty reinforced the commitment to environmental protection and its role in shaping and implementing environmental policy across Member States. The Treaty promoted the integration of environmental policies into other Community policies with environmental implications, including energy, transport, and regional development. The Treaty also reaffirmed key environmental principles such as the precautionary principle, the principle of preventive action, and the 'polluter pays' principle, that became foundational elements of EU environmental law and policy. The legal basis provided by the Treaty allowed the emergence of later key directives and regulations in areas such as air quality, water protection, waste management, and nature conservation (e.g. Natura 2000 Network on biodiversity and nature conservation, the Waste Framework Directive and the Water Framework Directive). The Treaty also supported the EU's global leadership in environmental negotiations and agreements, such as the United Nations Framework Convention on Climate Change (UNFCCC) and gave the EU external competence in environmental matters, allowing it to negotiate and conclude international agreements on behalf of its Member States.

1.4 The Treaty of Amsterdam

The Treaty of Amsterdam, signed in 1997 and entered into force in 1999, explicitly included sustainable development as an overarching objective.[17] It mandated the integration of environmental protection requirements into all sectoral policies (Article 6) to promote sustainable development and ensure that environmental protection is a cross-cutting principle in all EU policies. This treaty amended the Maastricht Treaty (Treaty on European Union) and the Treaty establishing the European Community to give greater prominence to environmental protection and sustainable development.

The Amsterdam Treaty also increased the European Parliament's influence over environmental legislation by extending the co-decision procedure to more areas, including environmental policy, and expanded the use of qualified majority voting (QMV) in the Council of Ministers for environmental matters. This move facilitated the adoption of environmental legislation by reducing the likelihood of individual

[16] https://www.europarl.europa.eu/factsheets/en/sheet/71/environment-policy-general-principles-and-basic-framework

[17] https://eur-lex.europa.eu/legal-content/EN/TXT/?uri=celex%3A11997D%2FTXT

Member States blocking proposals, thereby streamlining the legislative process. At the level of international environmental cooperation, the treaty reinforced the EU's role in international environmental governance and enabled the EU to negotiate and conclude international agreements on environmental protection more effectively. These changes provided a more robust legal and institutional framework for environmental protection and sustainability within the EU, laying the groundwork for subsequent environmental initiatives and legislation, such as the Directive on the Promotion of Renewable Energy Sources (2001)[18] and the Directive on Ambient Air Quality and Cleaner Air for Europe (2008).[19]

1.5 The Treaty of Lisbon

This Treaty, which came into force in December 2009, introduced several important provisions for the EU's environmental framework.[20] Article 3(3) mentions sustainable development as the basis for Europe's balanced economic growth, competitive social market economy, and for the protection and improvement of environment quality. In addition, Article 21(2)(f) specifies that the EU's external actions shall foster sustainable economic, social, and environmental development of developing countries, with the primary aim of eradicating poverty, which enhanced the EU's role in international environmental governance. The Treaty of Lisbon reinforced thus the integrated approach to environmental policy, by embedding environmental objectives and principles into the primary legislation of the EU across various articles, ensuring policy coherence and reducing the likelihood of conflicting policies. The explicit mention of climate change elevated its importance within the EU policy agenda and facilitated the development of subsequent climate strategies and action plans, such as the European Green Deal.

1.6 Strategies, Directives, and Action Plans

As noted earlier, environmental considerations got an increasing presence also beyond the EU treaties, in a wide range of strategies, directives, action plans initiatives, etc., implemented prior to the European Green Deal (Box 1.1).

[18] https://eur-lex.europa.eu/legal-content/EN/TXT/?uri=CELEX:32001L0077

[19] https://eur-lex.europa.eu/legal-content/EN/ALL/?uri=CELEX%3A32008L0050

[20] https://eur-lex.europa.eu/legal-content/EN/TXT/?uri=CELEX%3A12007L%2FTXT

Box 1.1 EU Climate Change Initiatives Prior to the European Green Deal

- *The Lisbon Strategy (2000)*, designed as an ambitious plan with wide-ranging economic and social reforms to make the EU the *"most competitive and dynamic knowledge-based economy in the world"*[21] was originally focused on two pillars—an economic one, for economic growth, employment, and knowledge-based economy, and a social one, for social cohesion, human resources and combating social exclusion. It was complemented in 2001 with a third pillar—an environmental one, called the *EU Sustainable Development Strategy (EU SDS)* (Bongardt & Torres, 2013) that held sustainable development as a central objective (climate change, public health, and natural resource management) but emphasised that economic growth should be decoupled from natural resource utilization. A 'renewed' EU SDS emerged in 2006, that was structured around seven key challenges to sustainable development, including climate change and clean energy. It included a new target related to green public procurement, setting the objective to achieve in 2010 an ' (Farmer, 2012, p. 3).
- *The EU Emissions Trading System*[22] *(ETS) (2005)* introduced the principle "the polluters pay for their greenhouse gas emissions" and the 'cap and trade' principle—a pioneering step in carbon pricing to reduce greenhouse gas emissions. The revenues from the pricing scheme primarily flow into national budgets of Member States, supporting investments in renewable energy, energy efficiency improvements and low-carbon technologies to further reduce emissions. These revenues also contribute to the EU ETS funds for low-carbon innovation and energy transition, the Innovation Fund and the Modernisation Fund. The ETS is currently in its fourth phase (2021–2030).
- *The Climate and Energy Package*[23] *2020 (2008)* set the three so-called "20-20-20" targets: (i) a 20% reduction in EU's Member States greenhouse gas emissions from 1990 levels by 2020; (ii) a 20% improvement in energy efficiency, and (iii) a 20% share of energy from renewable sources by 2020. The package was revised in 2014 as the *Climate and Energy Framework 2030,*[24] with new targets for the Member States by 2030: cut greenhouse gas emissions by 40%, produce at least 32% of energy from renewable energy sources and achieve at least 32.5% improvement in energy

(continued)

[21] https://www.europarl.europa.eu/summits/lis1_en.htm

[22] https://climate.ec.europa.eu/eu-action/eu-emissions-trading-system-eu-ets/what-eu-ets_en

[23] https://eur-lex.europa.eu/EN/legal-content/summary/2020-climate-and-energy-package.html

[24] https://www.consilium.europa.eu/en/policies/climate-change/2030-climate-and-energy-framework/

Box 1.1 (continued)

efficiency. These goals were included in the *2030 National Energy and Climate Plans (NECPs)* of the Member States outlining their climate and energy goals from 2021 to 2030.

- *The Renewable Energy Directive*[25] *(2009)* set binding national targets for increasing the share of renewable energy in the EU's energy mix, aiming for a 20% share of energy from renewable sources by 2020. A notable effect was the increase in the share of renewable energy sources in EU energy consumption from 12.5% in 2010 to 23% in 2022.[26] The directive was revised in 2023 to speed up the EU's clean energy transition.
- *Europe 2020: A strategy for smart, sustainable and inclusive growth (2010)*—a successor to the Lisbon Strategy—included climate change and energy among the five 'headline targets' for 2020 (European Commission, 2010).
- *The Energy Efficiency Directive*[27] *(2012)* introduced measures to enhance energy savings across sectors, including public buildings, industry, and transport to meet its energy efficiency headline target of 20% by 2020.
- *The 2030 Climate and Energy Framework*[28] *(2014)* aimed for a 40% reduction in greenhouse gas emissions, at least a 32% share for renewable energy, and a 32.5% improvement in energy efficiency by 2030.
- *The first Circular Economy Action Plan*[29] *(2015)* included 54 measures covering the whole life cycle: from production and consumption to waste management and the market for secondary raw materials and a revised legislative proposal on waste. The Plan set a vision for decoupling economic growth from resource use and environmental degradation.
- *The European Energy Union Strategy*[30] *(2015)* focuses on energy system integration and builds on the three key targets for the EU to meet by 2030: a minimum 40% cut in greenhouse gas emissions compared to 1990; at least a 27% market share for renewable energy; and an improvement in energy efficiency of not less than 27%.
- *The Going Climate-Neutral by 2050 strategy*[31] *(2018)* is based on seven strategic building blocks: energy efficiency, including zero emission

(continued)

[25] https://eur-lex.europa.eu/legal-content/EN/ALL/?uri=celex%3A32009L0028

[26] https://ec.europa.eu/eurostat/en/web/products-eurostat-news/w/ddn-20231222-2

[27] https://eur-lex.europa.eu/legal-content/EN/TXT/?uri=celex:32012L0027

[28] https://eur-lex.europa.eu/legal-content/EN/TXT/?uri=celex%3A52014DC0015R%2801%29

[29] https://eur-lex.europa.eu/legal-content/EN/TXT/?uri=CELEX:52015DC0614

[30] https://energy.ec.europa.eu/topics/energy-strategy/energy-union_en

[31] https://op.europa.eu/en/publication-detail/-/publication/92f6d5bc-76bc-11e9-9f05-01aa75ed71a1

Box 1.1 (continued)

buildings; increased use of renewables and of electricity to fully decarbonise Europe's energy supply; clean, safe and connected mobility; a competitive EU industry and the circular economy to reduce GHG emissions; smart network infrastructure and interconnections; bioeconomy and essential carbon sinks; and tackling remaining CO2 emissions with Carbon Capture and Storage (CCS).

Source: own selection

All the regulatory documents summarised above demonstrate that the EU had a robust framework of environmental policies and principles embedded in various treaties, strategies and initiatives well before the European Green Deal adoption in December 2019. These environmental policies and related activities at various EU institutional levels that began in the 1970s continued over the next decades, in an organic evolution. These policies increasingly integrated sustainability into broader economic and social frameworks, recognising the interdependence of environmental, economic and social goals.

What factors explain then the need for the European Green Deal? Evidence suggests that a set of compelling scientific, societal, policy and political factors converged in 2019, calling for advancing EU environmental policies to the next level. For instance, scientific evidence and reports from the Intergovernmental Panel on Climate Change (IPCC), the European Environment Agency, the European Climate Foundation, the OECD, etc., pointing to an accelerating pace of climate change and environmental degradation, penetrated deep into the mainstream political thinking and urged for immediate and more aggressive actions to mitigate the impacts. The Paris Agreement of December 2015 was a major catalyst, calling for more ambitious targets to limit global warming to well below 2°C, and preferably to 1.5°C, above pre-industrial levels. These targets required a higher integration of sustainability into economic and social policies, with a long-term roadmap and clear quantitative indicators that had not been in place before. At the societal level, citizen movements such as *Fridays for Future*, influenced public opinion and political agendas, demanding stronger climate action and sustainable policies both from the EU and the national governments. At the political level, Ursula von der Leyen's election in 2019 as President of the European Commission was pivotal. Her political platform included the European Green Deal as a flagship initiative, demonstrating strong political will at the highest level of EU leadership. Aiming to position itself as a global leader in climate action, the EU saw the European Green Deal as an instrument to assert geopolitical influence through environmental leadership. The synergy of these elements ensured that the European Green Deal was not just a product of the evolution of existing environmental policies but also a strategic and accelerated response to pressing contemporary challenges. These drivers will be examined in more detail in the next chapter.

References

Biermann, F., Davies, O., & van der Grijp, N. (2009). Environmental policy integration and the architecture of global environmental governance. *International Environmental Agreements, 9*, 351–369. https://doi.org/10.1007/s10784-009-9111-0

Bongardt, A., & Torres, F. (2013). Lisbon strategy. In E. Jones, A. Menon, & S. Weatherill (Eds.), *The Oxford handbook of the European Union*. (2012; online edition). Oxford Academic. https://doi.org/10.1093/oxfordhb/9780199546282.013.0033

Deters, H. (2019). European environmental policy at 50: Five decades of escaping decision traps? *Environmental Policy and Governance, 29*(5), 315–325. https://doi.org/10.1002/eet.1855

Domorenok, E. (2019). Voluntary instruments for ambitious objectives? The experience of the EU covenant of mayors. *Environmental Politics, 28*(2), 293–314. https://doi.org/10.1080/09644016.2019.1549777

European Commission. (2010). COM(2010) 2020 final. *EUROPE 2020 A strategy for smart, sustainable and inclusive growth*. https://op.europa.eu/en/publication-detail/-/publication/6a915e39-0aab-491c-8881-147ec91fe88a/language-hr

European Economic and Social Committee. (2012). *Opinion of the European Economic and Social Committee on the Seventh Environment Action Programme and follow-up to the sixth EAP (exploratory opinion)*. (2012/C 191/01). https://eur-lex.europa.eu/LexUriServ/LexUriServ.do?uri=OJ:C:2012:191:0001:0005:EN:PDF

European Environment Agency. (2020). *The European environment - state and outlook 2020. Knowledge for transition to a sustainable Europe*. https://www.eea.europa.eu//publications/soer-2020

Farmer, A. M. (Ed.). (2012). *Manual of European environmental policy*. Routledge. https://ieep.eu/wp-content/uploads/2022/12/1.7_The_SDS_Lisbon_Strategy_and_the_Europe_2020_Strategy_-_final.pdf

Hildebrand, P. M. (1992). The European community's environmental policy, 1957 to '1992': From incidental measures to an international regime? *Environmental Politics, 1*(4), 13–44. https://doi.org/10.1080/09644019208414044

Hofmann, A. (2019). Left to interest groups? On the prospects for enforcing environmental law in the European Union. *Environmental Politics, 28*(2), 342–364. https://doi.org/10.1080/09644016.2019.1549778

Knill, C., & Liefferink, D. (2007). *Environmental politics in the European Union: Policy-making, implementation and patterns of multi-level governance*. Manchester University Press.

Lenschow, A., & Sprungk, C. (2010). The myth of a green Europe. *Journal of Common Market Studies, 48*(1), 133–154. https://doi.org/10.1111/j.1468-5965.2009.02045.x

Machin, A. (2019). Changing the story? The discourse of ecological modernisation in the European Union. *Environmental Politics, 28*(2), 208–227. https://doi.org/10.1080/09644016.2019.1549780

Oberthür, S., & von Homeyer, I. (2022). From emissions trading to the European green deal: The evolution of the climate policy mix and climate policy integration in the EU. *Journal of European Public Policy, 30*(3), 445–468. https://doi.org/10.1080/13501763.2022.2120528

Rietig, K. (2019). The importance of compatible beliefs for effective climate policy integration. *Environmental Politics, 28*(2), 228–247.

Selin, H., & Van Deveer, S. D. (2015). Broader, deeper and greener: European Union environmental politics, policies, and outcomes. *Annual Review of Environment and Resources, 40*, 309–335. https://doi.org/10.1146/annurev-environ-102014-021210. https://home.cerge-ei.cz/richmanova/UPCES/SelinVanDeveerARER2015%20-%20European%20Union%20Environmental%20Policies%20and%20Outomes.pdf

Tsebelis, G., & Garrett, G. (2000). Legislative politics in the European Union. *European Union Politics, 1*(1), 9–36. https://doi.org/10.1177/1465116500001001002

Wurzel, R. K. W., Liefferink, D., & Di Lullo, M. (2019). The European Council, the Council and the Member States: Changing environmental leadership dynamics in the European Union. *Environmental Politics, 28*(2), 248–270. https://doi.org/10.1080/09644016.2019.1549783

Zito, A. R., Burns, C., & Lenschow, A. (2019). Is the trajectory of European Union environmental policy less certain? *Environmental Politics, 28*(2), 187–207. https://doi.org/10.1080/09644016.2019.1549779

Chapter 2
Key Drivers of the European Green Deal

Abstract The European Green Deal did not emerge solely from an organic evolution of the EU's environmental policies since the 1970s but was also a response to a nexus of scientific, societal, policy and political drivers that converged before December 2019 and required a strategic and accelerated reaction to pressing climate challenges. This chapter delves into these critical drivers, highlighting the variety of opinions and interests that paved the way for the European Green Deal.

In the decades leading up to the launch of the European Green Deal, several factors in the socio-economic and political landscape in Europe and globally urged for an accelerated response to environmental challenges. These include the growing body of scientific evidence from several sources on climate change and environmental degradation, the Paris Agreement's ambitious targets for reducing greenhouse gas emissions, the impact of social movements like 'Fridays for Future', which significantly raised public awareness and political pressure for climate action, and the EU's evolution as a global leader in climate change and sustainability. In this chapter, we take a closer look at these drivers, for a better understanding of their combined effects.

2.1 Scientific Evidence on the Climate Change and Environment Degradation

Scientific evidence on climate change and environmental degradation paving the way for the European Green Deal came from a variety of sources. Among them, the Intergovernmental Panel on Climate Change (IPCC) has been of key importance, due to its comprehensive reports synthesizing the latest scientific research on climate change, its impacts, and potential mitigation and adaptation strategies. The European Environment Agency (EEA) that provides detailed assessments of Europe's environment and the European Commission's Joint Research Centre (JRC)—the science and research arm of the Commission—have also been authoritative voices, as well as

M. Ranga, *Single Market 2.0*, Contributions to Economics,
https://doi.org/10.1007/978-3-031-83220-8_2

the International Energy Agency (IEA), the European Climate Foundation (ECF) and the World Meteorological Organization (WMO). There were also many scientific research papers in leading scientific journals, such as *Nature, Science* or peer-reviewed environmental journals that addressed climate change and environmental degradation. Let us now take a closer look at the evidence provided by these sources to better understand their impact.

The International Panel on Climate Change (IPCC)—the United Nations body for assessing the science related to climate change—has been a reference for climate change data and guiding global environmental policy since its inception in 1988 by the World Meteorological Organization (WMO) and the United Nations Environment Programme (UNEP).[1] With membership comprising governments of 195 countries that are members of the United Nations or the WMO, the IPCC brings together thousands of experts from all over the world to examine relevant scientific literature on the subject. They document the natural, economic and social impacts and risks, and compile the findings in scientific reports for national and international climate change policymaking and negotiations. The IPCC produces three types of reports: (i) comprehensive Assessment Reports on knowledge on climate change, its causes, potential impacts and response options; (ii) Special Reports, which assess specific issues; and (iii) Methodology Reports, which provide practical guidelines for the preparation of greenhouse gas inventories under the United Nations Framework Convention on Climate Change (UNFCCC). From the *First Assessment Report*[2] (1990) that highlighted the potential impacts of climate change and laid the groundwork for international climate policy, including the establishment of the UNFCCC, up to the *Fifth Assessment Report*[3] (2013–2014), the IPCC emphasised the anthropogenic causes of climate change and provided detailed projections of future climate change and its impacts, reinforcing the need for mitigation and adaptation. The Fifth Assessment Report was particularly influential in the negotiations leading up to the Paris Agreement, as it highlighted the severe risks and potential irreversible impacts of climate change, calling for urgent action. The *Special Report on Global Warming of 1.5°C* (IPCC, 2018) also stressed the differences in impact between 1.5°C and 2°C of warming, advocating for ambitious efforts to limit global temperature rise. Although the IPCC reports are often subject to criticism for their data, climate models, time frames and methodology that may overestimate or underestimate the impacts of climate change, or for being strongly influenced by political agendas, the overall reliability and influence of these reports on climate policy and action are well established.

The European Environment Agency (EEA) briefings and reports address single or systemic issues related to climate change.[4] An example is the *SOER 2015: European Environment—State and Outlook 2015* (European Environment Agency, 2015) that

[1] https://www.ipcc.ch/

[2] https://www.ipcc.ch/site/assets/uploads/2018/05/ipcc_90_92_assessments_far_contents.pdf

[3] https://www.ipcc.ch/assessment-report/ar5/2014/

[4] https://www.eea.europa.eu/en

examined the state of Europe's environment, trends, and prospects, and concluded that unsustainable systems of production and consumption need to be fundamentally rethought, and systemic solutions need to be found to recalibrate mobility, agriculture, energy, urban development, and other core systems to ensure the resilience of global natural systems. These conclusions have been further affirmed in the report *Climate Change Impacts and Vulnerability in Europe 2016* (European Environment Agency, 2016) that analysed observed and projected impacts of climate change on ecosystems, economy, human health and well-being across Europe and highlighted the increasing frequency and severity of extreme weather events and their socio-economic impacts. The report *Trends and Projections in Europe 2019: Tracking Progress Towards Europe's Climate and Energy Targets* (European Environment Agency, 2019) found that EU's progress towards its 2020 and 2030 climate and energy targets was too slow and the targets set for 2030 were still far to reach, urging for accelerated action from both the EU and the Member States to deliver collectively on their long-term objectives.

The European Commission's Joint Research Centre (JRC) contributes to climate change science that informs EU environmental policy in several ways. One of them are the annual *Global Energy and Climate Outlooks*[5] produced in collaboration with the European Commission's Directorate-General for Climate Action (DG CLIMA). For example, the *Global Energy and Climate Outlook 2018* (Keramidas et al., 2018) explored global transition pathways toward a low greenhouse gas (GHG) emissions economy, presenting scenarios compatible with the 2°C and 1.5°C temperature targets set by the UNFCCC Paris Agreement. The Outlook optimistically concluded that these targets are feasible provided that coordinated action is taken by all countries and sectors and can generate robust economic growth with minimal mitigation costs. Additionally, the Outlook argued that integration of climate and air quality policies could enhance air quality worldwide, supporting progress on the UN Sustainable Development Goals related to climate action, clean energy and good health. JRC also collects extensive data on climate variables for monitoring climate change trends and impacts and develops advanced models and simulation tools to assess the effectiveness of different mitigation and adaptation strategies. All this evidence supports climate policymaking by the European Commission and other EU institutions.

The International Energy Agency (IEA) has also produced evidence that laid the foundation for the European Green Deal, as part of its mission to offer analysis, data, policy recommendations and solutions to help countries provide secure and sustainable energy. An example is its *World Energy Outlook 2018* (IEA, 2018), which presents key data on global energy trends, carbon emissions of different sources of oil and gas, and the potential for renewable energy adoption, which contributed to shaping the energy policies in the European Green Deal.

The European Climate Foundation (ECF) is another voice that supported an overhaul of EU's climate policies. An example is the report *Net Zero by 2050: From*

[5] https://joint-research-centre.ec.europa.eu/scientific-activities-z/geco/past-geco-editions_en

Whether to How (European Climate Foundation, 2018) that used a simulation model of European emissions, outlining pathways to reach net-zero greenhouse gas (GHG) emissions in all sectors of the economy, influencing the ambitious targets set by the Green Deal.

The World Meteorological Organization[6] *(WMO)* provide *State of the Global Climate Reports,* which analyse climate trends, extreme weather events, and key indicators of climate change such as greenhouse gas concentrations, sea level rise, and ocean heat content.

2.2 The Paris Agreement and the Urge for More Ambitious and Integrated Climate Policies

The Paris Agreement, adopted by 196 parties at the COP21 conference in Paris in December 2015, played a crucial role in shaping the European Green Deal.[7] As a legally binding international treaty on climate change, it provided a global framework for climate action, with the main goal to keep the global average temperature rise well below 2°C above pre-industrial levels, with efforts to limit the increase to 1.5°C. This global commitment highlighted the urgency of climate action and placed significant pressure on the EU to align its climate policies with global targets and to lead by example.

Prior to COP21, the EU had already implemented a comprehensive array of climate initiatives on the home front, all emphasising the integration of climate and environmental concerns across various sectors and promoting essential policy concepts such as zero-emissions, circular economy and clean mobility (see Box 1.1 in Chap. 1). The *Seventh Environmental Action Plan* (2014–2020) that was already in operation had introduced the vision of transforming the EU into a resource-efficient, green and competitive low-carbon economy by 2020 and beyond to 2050, based on circular economy, biodiversity and sustainable management of resources. Complementing that, the EU's *Climate and Energy Framework 2030* (European Commission, 2014) and the *Going climate-neutral by 2050* strategy set new targets for the Member States by 2030 for energy efficiency and renewable energy (European Commission, 2019).

The new 2030 targets set by the European Commission have not been met with universal acclaim by governments, industry groups, think tanks, climate activists or the public. While many environmental organisations and climate activists welcomed the increased ambition, viewing the targets as a significant step forward in the fight against climate change, radical environmental groups and climate scientists criticised them for failing to address the climate challenges in an integrated and coherent manner across the industrial sectors or for not being ambitious enough. Among the

---

[6] https://wmo.int/

[7] https://unfccc.int/process-and-meetings/the-paris-agreement

Member States, some with strong environmental policies and progressive climate policies, such as Denmark, Sweden and the Netherlands, supported the ambitious targets and viewed them as an opportunity to lead by example and drive innovation in green technologies. In contrast, other Member States, particularly those heavily reliant on fossil fuels in Central and Eastern Europe, were concerned about the economic and social impacts, and called for more financial support and flexibility to achieve the targets. Also, some industry groups expressed concerns about the economic impact of the new targets, as potentially leading to higher costs for businesses and affecting competitiveness, especially in sectors like manufacturing and heavy industry. Other businesses, mainly those involved in renewable energy, electric vehicles and other green sectors, welcomed the targets as a driver for new investments and growth and as an opportunity to innovate and lead in the global market for clean technologies.

The criticism brought to these 2030 policies and the EU approach to the Paris Agreement commitments is particularly insightful, as it sheds light on the variety of opinions and interests that fuelled these intense debates. A brief review of academic and grey literature, along with contemporary press coverage identifies several key reasons for the discontent related to these policies:

- *Being too sectoral and fragmented:* The European Commission was criticised for lacking a unified, overarching strategy to integrate climate action with economic and social policies, failing to effectively address the multifaceted challenges of climate change and environmental degradation. Organisations such as the European Environmental Bureau (EEB), the Institute for European Environmental Policy (IEEP) and Bruegel contended that EU policies were often developed and implemented in isolation, with insufficient coordination and integration across different sectors such as energy, transport, agriculture and industry (Zachmann & Tagliapietra, 2018; European Environmental Bureau, 2019; Charveriat & Baldock, 2019; Charveriat & Kettunen, 2019). This siloed approach was considered a frequent source of conflicts between sectoral policies, duplication of efforts, missed opportunities for synergy and reduced overall effectiveness. The European Commission itself recognised the need for stronger integration of environmental policies with other social and economic policies to better achieve sustainable development goals in its *Reflection Paper. Towards a sustainable Europe by 2030* (European Commission, 2019a) (Box 2.1).

Box 2.1 Fragmentation of EU Environmental Policies

"Isolated, piecemeal approaches have proven to be ineffective. We need to formulate strategies that are comprehensive and integrated. For instance, environmental issues cannot be solved with environmental policies alone if economic policies continue to promote fossil fuels, resource inefficiency or unsustainable production and consumption. Similarly, social policies are not sufficient to accompany the fourth industrial revolution and support the labour

(continued)

Box 2.1 (continued)
force affected by the carbon-transition; strong education and training policies as well as research and development will be of crucial importance too to build the necessary resilience in our societies. Action is needed at all levels. [...] It is therefore of the utmost importance that all actors in the EU prioritise the sustainability transition. [...]. Significant parts of EU policies are already geared towards achieving the SDGs, but they still need to be put into practice in an integrated way by the Member States. [...] Policy coherence is a critical condition to ensure that we can deliver on the SDGs and ensure long-term green and inclusive growth for the EU."

Source: European Commission (2019a), p. 15

- *Insufficient ambition to effectively tackle climate change, too low emission reduction targets and weak enforcement mechanisms.* Critical voices on these topics included environmental NGOs such as Greenpeace, Friends of the Earth Europe, the European Environmental Bureau (EEB) and many others, who argued that the EU's climate policies did not go far enough to meet the urgent needs of climate science and failed to set high enough targets for emission reductions. Members of the European Parliament, particularly from the Green Party and other progressive groups, also voiced concerns about the Commission's climate policies, considering that the emission reduction targets were too conservative and that enforcement mechanisms lacked the necessary rigour to ensure compliance by Member States (Box 2.2). The European Court of Auditors highlighted other weaknesses in the implementation and enforcement of EU climate policies in several Special Reports. For instance, the 2017 Special Report *More efforts needed to implement the Natura 2000 network to its full potential* concluded that the implementation of Natura 2000 was incomplete and not effectively contributing to the EU's climate adaptation and mitigation efforts (European Court of Auditors, 2017). Also, the Special Report *EU greenhouse gas emissions: Well reported, but better insight needed into future reductions* found that while the EU had established a comprehensive framework for reporting greenhouse gas emissions, it lacked adequate insight into the effectiveness of policies and measures to achieve future emission reductions (European Court of Auditors, 2019).

Box 2.2 Insufficient Ambition and Underestimated Climate Targets of EU Environmental Policies
"Europe is playing well below its potential on climate change and Macron's empty words are not going to make a whole lot of difference. In Brussels, France fights much harder for its nuclear industry than for a transition to renewable energy and stands by while the likes of Spain and Poland seek

(continued)

Box 2.2 (continued)
subsidies for coal plants. Governments need to roll up their sleeves and get to work if Europe is to regain some of its credibility on climate change. They should start by raising the EU's 2030 targets to cut greenhouse gases and increase the share of renewable energy."

Source: Greenpeace European Unit (2017)

"A 50–55 percent emission cut by 2030 is not sufficient. Nature doesn't negotiate. The longer we wait to make the necessary changes in our economy, the more damage will be caused and the more difficult and expensive it will be. By delaying its proposal for the 2030 EU emissions reduction target to summer 2020, the Commission risks undermining the Paris agreement and any hope for EU climate leadership."

Source: Greenpeace European Unit (2019)

"EU leaders may pat themselves on the back for finally agreeing a new climate target, but this is still a far cry from the victory the climate needs. Our leaders must go further to deliver Europe's fair share of global action to cut carbon and live up to the agreement they made in Paris five years ago." (Colin Roche, climate justice coordinator for Friends of the Earth Europe).

Source: Taylor (2020)

"The 50.5–52.8% real emission reductions the Commission is proposing is grossly inadequate and completely irresponsible. Given the rapidly accelerating climate emergency, very rapid cuts in emissions are necessary. The UN emissions gap report 2019 implies a cut of at least 65% in EU emissions is needed to keep open the prospect of staying below 1.5 °C and so avoiding catastrophic impacts. [...] The Commission's proposal falls well short of this and risks the passing of dangerous tipping points in the climate system [...] The Commission's proposal to change the current 2030 target into a 'net' emissions target, including carbon sinks, is a serious mistake".

Source: Joint Declaration by the EEB and other climate NGOs (https://eeb.org/wp-content/uploads/2020/09/The-EU-2030-climate-target-_NGO-views.pdf)

"The modest 2030 targets are not in line with what the science tells us is needed to limit global warming to below 2 °C. After a promising start, Europe's climate ambitions are in fact sliding backwards again." (Rebecca Harms, co-chair of the Green Group in the European Parliament).

Source: Schiermeier (2014)

- *Insufficient drive of EU institutions in implementing environmental policies*: Several EU Member States, particularly those with more advanced environmental policies and ambitious national climate goals, such as Germany, Finland, Sweden, Denmark and the Netherlands, were particularly vocal about the slow implementation of EU's commitments under the Paris Agreement and the differences in the national enforcement mechanisms of climate policies. A broader belief emerged that existing policies and measures were insufficient to meet the goals and that more determined action from the EU institutions (the Commission, the Parliament and the EU Council) was needed to prevent the climate change consequences. Increasing pressure was being put on the EU institutions to align their policies with the goals of limiting global warming and transitioning to a low-carbon economy.

In fact, the European Parliament had already passed several regulations in the 2014–2019 period that covered a broad range of climate-related objectives,[8] e.g. to develop a fully integrated European energy market, strengthen the energy security, decarbonise the EU economy, increase solidarity and trust among the EU member states (European Parliament, 2019). These regulations asserted the commitment to advancing climate action and providing leadership on climate change mitigation within the EU and on the global stage, but their strength was considered insufficient.

A manifestation of the push exerted on the EU to adopt more ambitious climate targets, improve implementation of environmental policies and enforcement mechanisms was the formation of several 'green' coalitions. An example is the *Green Growth Group (GGG),* which brought together climate and environment ministers from 14 EU countries to influence EU climate and energy policy.[9] Their efforts contributed to the EU's decision to set a target of at least 40% reduction in greenhouse gas emissions by 2030 compared to 1990 levels. They also advocated for the EU's long-term climate strategy, which includes a roadmap for achieving net-zero greenhouse gas emissions by 2050, and promoted the use of carbon pricing and market-based instruments to reduce emissions, strengthening the EU Emissions Trading System (ETS). In the early 2010s, the ministers of the GGG joined the Corporate Leaders Group at the University of Cambridge and supportive members of the European Parliament to form the *Green Growth Partnership (GGP)*[10]—a forum for exchanges between progressive European governments and businesses on a climate-neutral Europe.

Lobbies were another manifestation of the political pressure on the European institutions to adopt stronger environmental policies and legislative action. An example is the *Memorandum to the Finnish Presidency of the European Union*

[8] For example, the *2030 Climate and Energy Framework Resolution* (2014) that called for binding targets for greenhouse gas emissions reduction, renewable energy, and energy efficiency by 2030; the *COP21 Follow-Up Resolution* (2016) issued after the adoption of the Paris Agreement calling for its swift implementation by EU member states; the *Carbon Market Reform Resolution* (2017) that called for reforms to the EU Emissions Trading System (ETS); the *Net-Zero Emissions Resolution* (2018) that called the EU to commit to achieving net-zero greenhouse gas emissions by 2050. In 2019, the *Climate Emergency Declaration* (November 2019) declared a climate emergency, urging the EC and EU member states to take immediate and concrete actions to address climate change.

[9] https://www.gov.uk/government/news/ministers-make-joint-case-for-ambitious-immediate-eu-low-carbon-action

[10] https://www.corporateleadersgroup.com/corporate-leaders-group-europe/green-growth-partnership

(European Environmental Bureau, 2019a) prepared by the European Environmental Bureau (EEB) in collaboration with the marine protection umbrella group Seas at Risk and presented to the Finnish Presidency of the EU at the start of their six-month mandate on 1 July 2019. The document summarised issues raised by the EEB Board, which has representatives from more than 30 countries and several European networks, into a ten-point action plan called *'Ten Green Tests'* (Box 2.3). The ten tests also constituted criteria for the assessment of the Finnish Presidency's performance at the end of its term in December 2019 (European Environmental Bureau, 2020). The assessment found that the Finnish Presidency of the EU made important progress in the areas of the European Green Deal, green finance, and climate change, but was less successful on the EU budget and the Common Agricultural Policy negotiations (Fig. 2.1).

Box 2.3 Ten Green Tests for the Finnish Presidency

"We call upon the Finnish Presidency of the European Union to promote a greener, more sustainable Europe, where our destructive impact on the climate, biodiversity and public health in Europe and beyond is rapidly decreased in line with citizens' expectations and scientific imperatives, through the following measures:

1. Recognise that there is a climate emergency and drive ambitious climate commitments to 1.5 degrees
2. Halt biodiversity loss: Protect our land and oceans
3. Transform food and farming systems through the Common Agricultural Policy
4. Make the EU Budget work for people and planet
5. Reduce air pollution to protect human health and the environment
6. Ensure clean and sufficient water for Europeans
7. Protect the public from hazardous chemicals
8. Transition to an innovative, resource efficient, circular economy
9. Strengthen democratic governance, the rule of law and environmental justice
10. Implement the Sustainable Development Goals and commit to a transformative 8EAP"

Source: selected from European Environmental Board (2019a)

2.3 Pressure of Social Movements

Several weekly climate strikes took place in 2018 and 2019, engaging millions of people in more than 150 countries around the world (BBC, 2019; CNN, 2019) and marking a key moment for young people's climate activism (Pickard et al., 2020; Neas et al., 2022). The protests were organised by young people participating in the

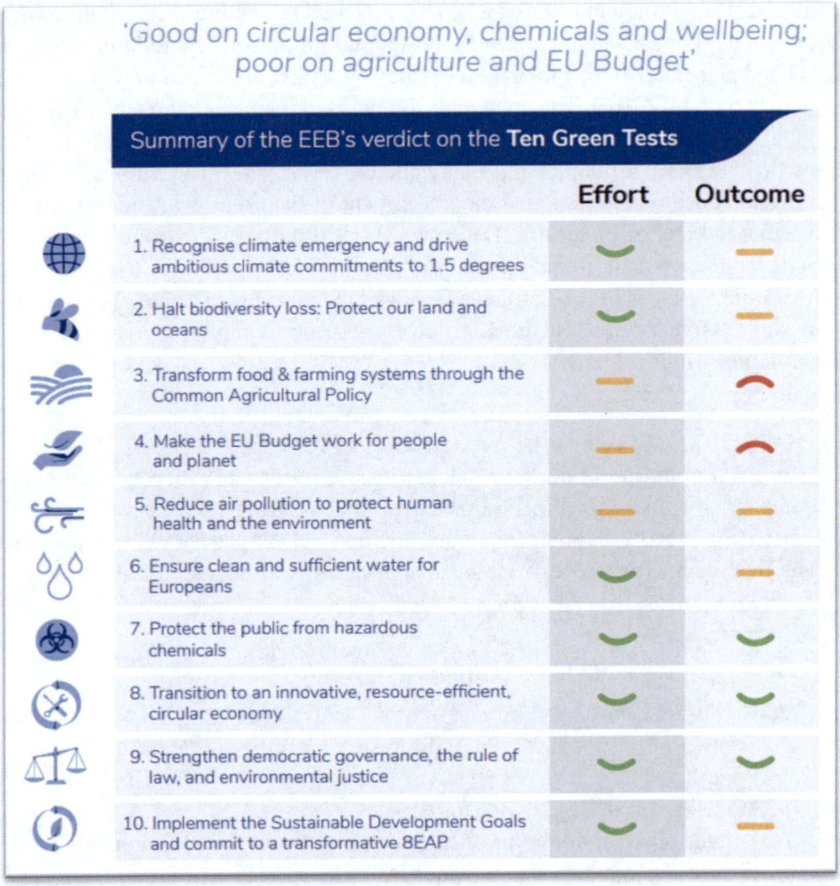

Fig. 2.1 The EEB's assessment of the environmental performance of the Finnish Presidency of the EU, July—December 2019. Based on the EEB's *Ten Green Tests* for the Finnish Presidency released in June 2019. Source: European Environmental Board (2020), p. 3

'Fridays for Future' campaigns—the youth-led and organised climate movement inspired by Greta Thunberg's mass protests for three weeks in front of the Swedish Parliament.[11] The climate strikes were motivated by a variety of factors, from the discontent with government actions to mitigate climate change and design adequate policies and targets, to the demand for systemic change, the concern about the future impacts of climate change on their lives and the planet, and a global solidarity, showing that climate change is a universal issue requiring collective action.

[11] https://fridaysforfuture.org/

These youth-led social protests had an unprecedented political and media impact, raising public awareness about the urgent need for climate action and placing substantial pressure on political leaders and policymakers to prioritise climate action and environmental sustainability. The visibility and urgency of the 'Fridays for Future' campaigns made it clear that climate change was a top priority for many European citizens, particularly the younger generation, and helped the protesters translate some of their demands into clear policy pledges and initiatives for new targets for the reduction of CO2 emissions (Sloam et al., 2022). The protests revealed an increasing engagement of young people in climate activism and advocacy and demonstrated that environmental issues rose to the top of young people's priorities, in conjunction with a growth in 'cosmopolitan values' (Kitanova, 2019; Sloam & Henn, 2019; Pickard, 2022).

The 'Fridays for Future' campaigns catalysed the adoption of more ambitious climate policies in the EU and prompted a shift in the policymakers' political discourse, by framing climate change as an immediate crisis rather than a distant future problem. Climate action rose to the top of the EU's political agenda, with both the European Commission and national governments recognising the need to respond to the growing public demand for more ambitious climate policies. European leaders and policymakers, including Ursula von der Leyen, the President of the European Commission, publicly acknowledged the influence of youth climate activists and pledged to implement more comprehensive and integrated climate policies (Jack, 2022).

2.4 Asserting Global Leadership in Climate Change and Sustainability

The EU pursued global leadership in climate change and sustainability since these concerns rose to prominence in international politics in the 1990s. This leadership role was seen as crucial not only for influencing global policies but also for enhancing EU's competitiveness in the global market, particularly in the burgeoning field of green technologies. The bloc demonstrated early leadership already in the 1990s, as a strong supporter of the 1992 UN Framework Convention on Climate Change (UNFCCC) and the 1997 Kyoto Protocol that committed industrialised countries and economies in transition to limit greenhouse gases (GHG) emissions in accordance with agreed individual targets.[12]

Despite strong opposition from the USA (President George W. Bush refused to ratify the Kyoto Protocol, in disagreement with its legally binding targets, continuing the opposition shown shortly after taking office, by formally withdrawing USA support for the treaty, stating that it would hurt the economy, especially industries reliant on fossil fuels, and that the agreement placed unfair burdens on the USA, while

[12] https://unfccc.int/kyoto_protocol

allowing large developing economies to avoid binding emissions cuts), the EU showcased significant leadership by persuading the international community to advance without the USA, taking a calculated risk, as there was no assurance that other nations would follow suit. Nevertheless, the EU succeeded in making the Kyoto Protocol a functioning agreement and met the crucial requirement that the total number of signatories be responsible for at least 55% of global greenhouse gas emissions (Barichella, 2017). During the Kyoto Protocol's first commitment period (2008–2012), participating countries committed to reducing emissions by an average of 5% below 1990 levels, but the EU's 15 member countries at the time (EU15) went beyond this and committed to an 8% reduction for the entire bloc. The overall 8% reduction was broken down into legally binding national targets for each Member State, tailored to their relative wealth, and the EU15 reported an overall cut of 11.7% domestically at the end of the first commitment period.[13]

In the first decade of the 2000s, the EU strengthened its global influence by playing an active role in several international events that paved the way to the 2015 Paris Agreement, such as the Bali Action Plan (2007), the Copenhagen Summit (2009) and the Durban Platform (2011), where it advocated for a legally binding global climate deal, stronger international commitments and more ambitious climate action. The EU was also a key player in securing the Paris Agreement (2015), facilitating negotiations between developed and developing countries and bridging the development needs of the global South with the more stringent climate demands of the developed North. In a strong commitment, the EU and all its Member States signed and ratified the Paris Agreement and set the goal to become the world's first climate-neutral economy and society by 2050, pledging to reduce EU emissions by at least 55% by 2030, compared to 1990 levels.[14]

After the Paris Agreement, the EU continued to assert its leadership in global climate policy, despite the US withdrawal from the accord in June 2017 further to President Trump's decision. The EU took several key steps to advance its climate goals and uphold the commitments made in Paris, considering the accord as 'an opportunity for Europe to redouble internal efforts to implement current climate commitments and perhaps even surpass them. This is essential in order to send a strong signal to other countries that Europe is determined to assume a key role in safeguarding the accord' (Barichella, 2017).

The EU's most comprehensive response to the Paris Agreement was the adoption of the European Green Deal in December 2019. It came with new targets to achieve climate neutrality by 2050, with comprehensive legislative measures, and with substantial financial commitments to ensure these targets were met. On the international stage, the EU kept the momentum of the Paris Agreement alive by building coalitions with other countries and regions committed to climate action and providing support to developing countries for climate mitigation and adaptation efforts.

[13] https://climate.ec.europa.eu/eu-action/international-action-climate-change/kyoto-1st-commitment-period-2008-12_en

[14] https://www.consilium.europa.eu/en/policies/climate-change/paris-agreement/#gsc-main-content

The EU's steadfast commitment was a crucial factor in maintaining the integrity and momentum of the Paris Agreement until the USA rejoined under President Biden in 2021.

Along this diplomatic journey, the EU's performance evolved from the policy interventions of the 1990s and early 2000s, where it took primarily a negotiator role for progressive climate action and a 'green normative power' oriented on impartiality, belief in multilateralism, sustainable development and the precautionary principle, to a more ambitious and proactive leadership role, supporting the Paris Agreement and favouring mutual recognition and non-domination policies and instruments (Van Schaik & Schunz, 2012; von Lucke, 2021).

This evolution from a regional leader to a major international advocate for climate action suggests a shift towards a 'leadiator'—mediator-cum-leadership position—characterised by greater emphasis on coalition and bridge-building, coordination of EU institutions and stronger integration of domestic and international climate policies (Bäckstrand & Elgström, 2013; Oberthür & Dupont, 2021). This shift includes an increasing integration of climate diplomacy into the EU's broader foreign policy agenda, mainstreaming climate issues across various policy areas, such as trade, development cooperation, energy and security, and recognising climate change as a cross-cutting global challenge.

Part of that evolution was due to some distinctive forms of contestation within the EU of energy security (security of supply, climate security and wider security challenges), reflecting broader geopolitical imperatives (Youngs, 2020). Additionally, there has been a growing convergence of views among EU Member States, leading to more unified and coherent climate diplomacy and internal consensus. This was further supported by EU's expanding engagement with non-state actors such as civil society organizations and businesses in climate diplomacy, which mobilised support for climate action and enhanced the EU's influence and credibility on the global stage. The EU strengthened its relations with developing countries by providing financial and technical assistance and ensuring accountability and transparency in climate action efforts. For example, the *High-Level Expert Group on Sustainable Finance* was established in 2016, bringing together 20 senior experts from civil society, the finance sector, academia and observers from European and international institutions to advise the European Commission on steering public and private capital towards sustainable investments.[15] The EU has also provided substantial financial and technical support to developing countries to help them transition to sustainable energy systems and adapt to climate change impacts through many programmes that have been critical in building trust and cooperation in international climate negotiations. One of the most important financial support schemes for the developing countries is the *EU External Investment Plan (EIP)*[16]—a flagship initiative launched in 2017 to attract investment for sustainable

[15] https://finance.ec.europa.eu/publications/high-level-expert-group-sustainable-finance-hleg_en

[16] https://international-partnerships.ec.europa.eu/funding-and-technical-assistance/funding-instruments/guarantees-and-blending_en

development, including green projects, particularly from businesses and private investors, into countries neighbouring the EU (EU Neighbourhood) and in Africa. The *Global Climate Change Alliance Plus (GCCA+)*[17] is another EU flagship initiative that has been operational since 2007 and provides funding and technical assistance for climate adaptation and mitigation in vulnerable countries in Africa, Asia, the Caribbean and the Pacific. Other partnerships specifically focused on energy are the Africa-EU Energy Partnership (AEEP), EU-Pacific Alliance for Sustainable Energy and the EU-ASEAN Energy Cooperation.

References

Bäckstrand, K., & Elgström, O. (2013). The EU's role in climate change negotiations: From leader to 'leadiator'. *Journal of European Public Policy, 20*(10), 1369–1386. https://doi.org/10.1080/13501763.2013.781781

Barichella, A. (2017, November 6). *How Europe can and should become the guardian of the Paris Agreement on climate change?* Fondation Robert Schuman. Schuman Papers and Interviews: Schuman Paper no. 450. https://www.robert-schuman.eu/en/european-issues/0450-how-europe-can-and-should-become-the-guardian-of-the-paris-agreement-on-climate-change

BBC. (2019, September 21). *Climate protests: Marches worldwide against global warming*. https://www.bbc.com/news/world-49777279

Charveriat, C. & Baldock, D. (2019, November 4). *Reinventing growth for Europe: Time for a paradigm shift.* Institute for Environmental Public Policy. https://ieep.eu/news/reinventing-growth-for-europe-time-for-a-paradigm-shift/

Charveriat, C. & Kettunen, M. (2019, November 9). *Time to get real about sustainability and trade within the European Green Deal.* Institute for Environmental Public Policy. https://ieep.eu/news/time-to-get-real-about-sustainability-and-trade-within-the-european-green-deal/

CNN. (2019, September 20). *Teen activist tells protesters demanding action on climate change: 'We need to do this now.'* https://edition.cnn.com/2019/09/20/world/global-climate-strike-september-intl/index.html

European Commission. (2014). *COM(2014) 15 final/2 A policy framework for climate and energy in the period from 2020 to 2030.* https://data.consilium.europa.eu/doc/document/ST%205644%202014%20REV%201/EN/pdf

European Commission. (2019). *Going climate-neutral by 2050 – A strategic long-term vision for a prosperous, modern, competitive and climate-neutral EU economy.* Directorate-General for Climate Action, Publications Office. https://data.europa.eu/doi/10.2834/02074

European Commission. (2019a). *Reflection Paper. Towards a sustainable Europe by 2030.* https://commission.europa.eu/publications/sustainable-europe-2030_en#description

European Court of Auditors. (2017). *Special Report 01/2017 - More efforts needed to implement the Natura 2000 network to its full potential.* https://www.eca.europa.eu/Lists/ECADocuments/SR17_1/SR_NATURA_2000_EN.pdf

European Court of Auditors. (2019). *Special report no 18/2019: EU greenhouse gas emissions: Well reported, but better insight needed into future reductions.* https://www.eca.europa.eu/en/publications?did=51834

European Environment Agency. (2015). *SOER 2015 — The European environment — state and outlook 2015.* https://www.eea.europa.eu/soer/2015

[17] https://capacity4dev.europa.eu/groups/gcca-community/info/1-about-gcca_en

European Environment Agency. (2016). *Climate change impacts and vulnerability in Europe 2016.* https://www.eea.europa.eu/publications/climate-change-impacts-and-vulnerability-2016

European Environment Agency. (2019). *Trends and projections in Europe 2019. Tracking progress towards Europe's climate and energy targets.* https://www.eea.europa.eu/publications/trends-and-projections-in-europe-1

European Environmental Bureau. (2019). *Open letter to EU leaders: Our sustainable future must start now.* https://eeb.org/open-letter-sustainable-future-now/.

European Environmental Bureau. (2019a). *Memorandum to the Finnish Presidency of the European Union. Prepared in cooperation with Seas at Risk.* https://eeb.org/memo-to-finnish-presidency/

European Environmental Bureau. (2020). *The EEB's Assessment of the environmental performance of the Finnish Presidency of the EU. July–December 2019. Prepared in cooperation with Seas at Risk.* https://eeb.org/wp-content/uploads/2020/01/Assessment-FI-2019-1.pdf

European Parliament. (2019). *The Juncker Commission's ten priorities: An end-of-term assessment.* European Parliament. https://www.europarl.europa.eu/RegData/etudes/IDAN/2019/637943/EPRS_IDA(2019)637943_EN.pdf

Greenpeace European Unit. (2017, December 12). *Greenpeace comment on One Planet climate summit.* Press release. https://www.greenpeace.org/eu-unit/issues/climate-energy/971/greenpeace-comment-on-one-planet-climate-summit/

Greenpeace European Unit. (2019, December 11). *European Green Deal misses the mark.* https://www.greenpeace.org/eu-unit/issues/climate-energy/2517/european-green-deal-misses-the-mark/

IEA. (2018). *World energy outlook 2018.* IEA. https://www.iea.org/reports/world-energy-outlook-2018. Licence: CC BY 4.0

IPCC. (2018). *Special report. Global warming of 1.5 °C.* https://www.ipcc.ch/sr15/

Jack, V. (2022, March 26). *Von der Leyen meets youth climate activists to talk about Russian energy.* Politico. https://www.politico.eu/article/von-der-leyen-meets-youth-climate-activists-to-talk-about-russian-energy/

Keramidas, K., Tchung-Ming, S., Diaz-Vazquez, A. R., Weitzel, M., Vandyck, T., Després, J., Schmitz, A., Rey Los Santos, L., Wojtowicz, K., Schade, B., Saveyn, B., & Soria-Ramirez, A. (2018). *Global energy and climate outlook 2018: Sectoral mitigation options towards a low-emissions economy – Global context to the EU strategy for long-term greenhouse gas emissions reduction, EUR 29462 EN.* Publications Office of the European Union, , ISBN 978-92-79-97462-5. https://doi.org/10.2760/67475.JRC113446

Kitanova, M. (2019). Youth political participation in the EU: Evidence from a cross-national analysis. *Journal of Youth Studies, 23*(7), 819–836. https://doi.org/10.1080/13676261.2019.1636951

Neas, S., Ward, A., & Bowman, B. (2022). Young people's climate activism: A review of the literature. *Frontiers Political Science, Section Political Participation, 4.* https://doi.org/10.3389/fpos.2022.940876

Oberthür, S., & Dupont, C. (2021). The European Union's international climate leadership: Towards a grand climate strategy? *Journal of European Public Policy, 28*(7), 1095–1114. https://doi.org/10.1080/13501763.2021.1918218

Pickard, S. (2022). Young environmental activists and do-it-ourselves (DIO) politics: Collective engagement, generational agency, efficacy, belonging and hope. *Journal of Youth Studies, 25*(6), 730–750. https://doi.org/10.1080/13676261.2022.2046258

Pickard, S., Bowman, B., & Arya, D. (2020). "We are radical in our kindness": The political socialisation, motivations, demands and protest actions of young environmental activists in Britain. *Youth Globalization, 2*, 251–280. https://doi.org/10.1163/25895745-02020007

Schiermeier, Q. (2014, January 22). *'Modest' EU climate targets criticized.* Nature. https://doi.org/10.1038/nature.2014.14573.

Sloam, J., & Henn, M. (2019). *Youthquake 2017: The rise of young cosmopolitans in Britain.* Palgrave Macmillan.

Sloam, J., Pickard, S., & Henn, M. (2022). Young people and environmental activism: The transformation of democratic politics. *Journal of Youth Studies, 25*(6), 683–691. https://doi.org/10.1080/13676261.2022.2056678

Taylor, K. (2020, December 15). *Reactions: Deal on EU's 2030 climate target is a big step, but won't close the gap to 2050.* Euractiv. https://www.euractiv.com/section/energy-environment/news/55-reduction-is-a-big-step-but-wont-close-the-gap-to-2050/

Van Schaik, L., & Schunz, S. (2012). Explaining EU activism and impact in global climate politics: Is the union a norm- or interest-driven actor? *Journal of Common Market Studies, 50*(1), 169–186. https://doi.org/10.1111/j.1468-5965.2011.02214.x

von Lucke, F. (2021). Principled pragmatism in climate policy? The EU and changing practices of climate justice. *Political Geography, 86*, 102355. https://doi.org/10.1016/j.polgeo.2021.102355

Youngs, R. (2020). EU foreign policy and energy strategy: Bounded contestation. *Journal of European Integration, 42*(1), 147–162. https://doi.org/10.1080/07036337.2019.1708345

Zachmann, G. & Tagliapietra, S. (2018, April 9). *Addressing Europe's failure to clean up the transport sector.* Policy brief. Bruegel. https://www.bruegel.org/policy-brief/addressing-europes-failure-clean-transport-sector

Chapter 3
Novel Features of the European Green Deal

Abstract This chapter examines the three structural pillars of the European Green Deal: a comprehensive package of over 50 proposals across key economic sectors, measures to establish the EU as a global leader in the green transition, and the launch of a European Climate Pact to engage citizens. Novel features of the package include a holistic, higher-level integration of environmental sustainability across all EU policies, ambitious legally binding targets, and unprecedented financial investments, including the Just Transition Mechanism to support regions most affected by the transition. While widely praised for its visionary and ambitious approach, the European Green Deal has also faced criticism for its perceived lack of ambition, protectionist tendencies and uneven policy implementation, reflecting the variety of opinions and challenges in reshaping Europe's environmental, social and economic landscapes.

The European Green Deal adopted in December 2019 in response to a worsening climate and environmental crisis and as a strategy to achieve the United Nation's 2030 Sustainable Development goals, posited a 'commitment to tackling climate and environmental-related challenges that is this generation's defining task' (European Commission, 2019). The European Green Deal presented itself as 'a new growth strategy that aims to transform the EU into a fair and prosperous society, with a modern, resource-efficient and competitive economy where there are no net emissions of greenhouse gases in 2050 and where economic growth is decoupled from resource use' (ibid.) With its dual aim to transform the EU's economy *and* society, the European Green Deal has been met with both acclaim for its ambitious vision, sense of pride and monumental achievements and pointed criticism for not being ambitious enough in tackling environmental challenges, for protectionist measures and uneven policy focus. In this chapter, we explore the innovations introduced by the European Green Deal and analyse the factors contributing to its mixed reception.

M. Ranga, *Single Market 2.0*, Contributions to Economics,
https://doi.org/10.1007/978-3-031-83220-8_3

3.1 Structure of the European Green Deal and Novel Features

The European Green Deal structure relies on three main pillars of its ambitious goals:

1. *A comprehensive package of over 50 proposals for strategies, initiatives, action plans,* etc. *supporting the EU's climate ambition through transformative policies in key economic sectors.* The package is accompanied by a roadmap (Table 3.1) with timelines for each policy proposal to be developed by the European Commission and the Member States' national governments in the subsequent months and years through dedicated strategies. Sustainability took centre stage, as it was acknowledged as a formal objective in all EU policies and national policies of the Member States and was backed by dedicated 'green' investments channelled through the Sustainable Europe Investment Plan and a specific Just Transition Fund 'to leave no one behind'. The European Investment Bank Group, national promotional banks and institutions, as well as other international financial institutions and private investors were called to provide green finance and increase the use of green budgeting tools. Strong emphasis was placed on research and innovation to develop and implement clean technologies and other new technologies across the Single Market, building new innovative value chains. Education and training for green purposes were also mentioned as key areas for support through dedicated measures, such as a European competence framework to help develop and assess knowledge, skills and attitudes on climate change and sustainable development. The novel principle of 'do no harm' was introduced as a commitment of all EU actions and policies to pull together to help the EU achieve a successful and just green transition.
2. *Measures for establishing the EU as a global leader in the transition to a green economy,* by promoting through stronger 'green deal diplomacy' and leading by example, mobilising both bilateral and multilateral diplomatic channels (e.g. the United Nations, the G7, the G20, the World Trade Organisation and other relevant international fora) to enhance the EU's geopolitical distinction.
3. *Launch of a European Climate Pact,* reflecting the European Commission's commitment to involve citizens in the design and implementation of 'green' transition policies. Expected by March 2020, the European Climate Pact envisioned three engagement strategies: (i) to inform, inspire and create citizens' awareness of climate change and environmental threats through various channels, such as citizens' dialogues and assemblies, social dialogue committees, energy communities and dedicated events in the Member States; (ii) to create physical and virtual spaces for people to share ideas, collaborate on ambitious actions and commit to specific climate goals; and (iii) to build capacity for grassroots climate initiatives by providing information, guidance and educational modules to facilitate good practices.

This comprehensive package proposed by the European Green Deal brought several novel elements relative to previous EU 'green' policies:

Table 3.1 Roadmap—key actions of the European Green Deal

Actions	Indicative Timetable
Climate Ambition	
Proposal on a European 'Climate Law' enshrining the 2050 climate neutrality objective	March 2020
Comprehensive plan to increase the EU 2030 climate target to at least 50% and towards 55% in a responsible way	Summer 2020
Proposals for revisions of relevant legislative measures to deliver on the increased climate ambition, following the review of emissions trading system directive; effort sharing regulation; land use, land use change and forestry regulation; energy efficiency directive; renewable energy directive; CO2 emissions performance standards for cars and vans	June 2021
Proposal for a revision of the energy taxation directive	June 2021
Proposal for a carbon border adjustment mechanism for selected sectors	2021
New EU Strategy on adaptation to climate change	2020/2021
Clean, affordable and secure energy	
Assessment of the final national energy and climate plans	June 2020
Strategy for smart sector integration	2020
'Renovation wave' initiative for the building sector	2020
Evaluation and review of the Trans-European Network—Energy Regulation	2020
Strategy on offshore wind	2020
Industrial strategy for a clean and circular economy	
EU industrial strategy	March 2020
Circular economy action plan, including a sustainable products initiative and particular focus on resource intense sectors such as textiles, construction, electronics and plastics	March 2020
Initiatives to stimulate lead markets for climate neutral and circular products in energy intensive industrial sectors	From 2020
Proposal to support zero carbon steel-making processes by 2030	2020
Legislation on batteries in support of the Strategic Action Plan on Batteries and the circular economy	October 2020
Propose legislative waste reforms	From 2020
Sustainable and smart mobility	
Strategy for sustainable and smart mobility	2020
Funding call to support the deployment of public recharging and refuelling points as part of alternative fuel infrastructure	From 2020
Assessment of legislative options to boost the production and supply of sustainable alternative fuels for the different transport modes	From 2020
Revised proposal for a directive on combined transport	2021
Review of the alternative fuels infrastructure directive and the TEN-transport regulation	2021
Initiatives to increase and better manage the capacity of railways and inland waterways	From 2021
Proposal for more stringent air pollutant emissions standards for combustion-engine vehicles	2021
Greening the Common Agricultural Policy/'Farm to Fork' strategy	

(continued)

Table 3.1 (continued)

Actions	Indicative Timetable
Examination of the draft national strategic plans, with reference to the ambitions of the European Green Deal and the 'Farm to Fork' strategy	2020–2021
'Farm to Fork' strategy. Measures, including legislative, to significantly reduce the use and risk of chemical pesticides, as well as the use of fertilisers and antibiotics	Spring 2020 2021
Preserving and protecting biodiversity	
EU Biodiversity Strategy for 2030	March 2020
Measures to address the main drivers of biodiversity loss	From 2021
New EU forest strategy	2020
Measures to support deforestation-free value chains	From 2020
Towards a zero-pollution ambition for a toxic free environment	
Chemicals strategy for sustainability	Summer 2020
Zero pollution action plan for water, air and soil	2021
Revision of measures to address pollution from large industrial installations	2021
Mainstreaming sustainability in all EU policies	
Proposal for a Just Transition Mechanism, including a Just Transition Fund, and a Sustainable Europe investment plan	January 2020
Renewed sustainable finance strategy	Autumn 2020
Review of the non-financial reporting directive	2020
Initiatives to screen and benchmark green budgeting practices of the Member States and the EU	From 2020
Review of the relevant State aid guidelines, including environment and energy State aid guidelines	2021
Align all new Commission initiatives with the Green Deal objectives and promote innovation	From 2020
Stakeholders to identify and remedy incoherent legislation that reduces the effectiveness in delivering the European Green Deal	From 2020
Integration of the Sustainable Development Goals in the European Semester	From 2020
The EU as a Global Leader	
EU to continue to lead the international climate and biodiversity negotiations	From 2019
Strengthen the EU's Green Deal Diplomacy in cooperation with Member States	From 2020
Bilateral efforts to induce partners to act and to ensure comparability of action and policies	From 2020
Green Agenda for the Western Balkans	From 2020
Working Together—A European Climate Pact	
Launch of the European Climate Pact	March 2020
Proposal for an 8th Environmental Action Programme	2020

Source: European Commission (2019). Annex to the Communication on the European Green Deal 'Roadmap—Key actions'

Source: green_deal_birthday_tree_en.pdf (europa.eu)

Fig. 3.1 Sectoral approach of the European Green Deal. Source: green_deal_birthday_tree_en.pdf (europa.eu)

- *A holistic approach, introducing environmental sustainability as the central axis for integrating climate policy into key economic and social sectors*

To ensure an integrated vision of the transition to a more resource-efficient and technologically advanced EU economy, the European Green Deal goes beyond the 'traditional' environmental policy areas (biodiversity, air quality, water management, waste, chemicals) and addresses the interconnected nature of environmental, economic, and social challenges, going deep into key economic sectors (Fig. 3.1).

Environmental sustainability appears as the central axis for integrating environmental, economic and social concerns and represents a distinctive element of the new approach.

While the integration of environmental policy across other economic sectors is not new, as it has been affirmed in many EU treaties and strategies before the European Green Deal (see Chap. 1 for details), it has not been applied consistently, especially in sectors in which conflicting policy objectives take precedence over environment/climate, such as 'energy security' in energy policy (Monta, 2020).

Schunz (2022) identifies environmental sustainability as a significant discursive break and a paradigm shift relative to preceding Lisbon Strategy and Europe 2020, which is legitimised in all policy areas, from EU and national policymakers' mandates to actions of pro-environmental organisations and civil society. Moreover, sectoral policies (e.g. trade) are now expected to contribute to attaining environmental objectives, and not the other way round, as stipulated by the Lisbon Strategy and Europe 2020 when referring to eco-efficiency as a driver of growth (ibid.) Molek-Kozakowska (2023) also remarks the central place of environmental sustainability in the European Green Deal and its role as an attribute to 'jobs and growth', in a change of discourse that aims to *"normalise 'sustainability' as the contingency between environmental and economic orders of discourse. This …ideological hybridity also sheds light onto how EU institutions are (self)authorised to lead actions on environmental challenges on behalf of European citizens"* (p. 182). The European Green Deal not only expands the climate policy integration into virtually all policy sectors initiatives, with environmental issues taking priority over sectoral objectives, but also comes with a whole new set of policy instruments that enhance sectoral differentiation and specialisation of EU climate policy, ultimately strengthening climate governance and making climate policy framework more effective (Oberthür & von Homeyer, 2022).

- *Ambitious targets and legally binding provisions*

As shown in Chap. 1, climate governance targets have been established by the EU in a wide range of policies that have been implemented over the last two decades (see Box 1.1 in Chap. 1 for details on the specific targets). With the proposal for a European Climate Law, the European Green Deal took a firm step forward by enshrining the overall 2030 emission reduction target of 55% and the 2050 climate-neutrality target in law. Indeed, the first European Climate Law (European Parliament and the Council of the European Union, 2021) adopted in 2021 turned the political ambition of reaching climate neutrality by 2050 into a legal obligation for the EU and set the intermediate target of reducing net greenhouse gas emissions by at least 55% by 2030, compared to 1990 levels.

Considered by many as a real 'game changer' (e.g. Mathieu, 2021), the law placed climate at the heart of all EU policymaking, opening the way for a wide range of future regulations to support the emissions-cutting aims. The National Energy and Climate Plans (NECPs) that had been introduced in 2019, prior to the Climate Law, as a requirement for the Member States to supply clean, affordable and secure energy by end 2019, had to be updated in 2023, introducing thus the Member States' obligation to perform coherent and mutually supportive actions and strategies. The European Commission took the right to monitor the implementation and consistency of national and EU measures and launched independent climate advisory bodies both at the EU level—the European Scientific Advisory Board on Climate Change—and at the level of the national authorities of the Member States. The law also introduced a mechanism to calculate the total emissions the EU can produce from 2030 to 2050, under its climate targets. These legally binding targets for reducing greenhouse gas emissions provided a roadmap for the EU Member States and accelerated the pace of emissions reductions and renewable energy deployment. The European Climate Law was complemented in 2020 by the *European Climate Pact* (European Commission,

2020) that was designed as a social movement for building a more sustainable Europe.

The European Green Deal proposal package introduced many other ambitious objectives that were materialised in March 2020, such as the *New Industrial Strategy for Europe* (European Commission, 2020a), *A new Circular Economy Action Plan For a cleaner and more competitive Europe* (European Commission, 2020b) and the *Renovation Wave for Europe—greening our buildings, creating jobs, improving lives* (European Commission, 2020c) that provides principles for building renovation towards 2030 and 2050.

- *Large-scale financial investment and innovative use of financing and reporting mechanisms*

To realise its objectives, the European Gren Deal mobilised unprecedented levels of public investment. Initial estimates indicated at least EUR one trillion over the 2021–2030 decade to be mobilised from EU and national public budgets, as well as the private sector,[1] but updated estimates suggested higher annual investments by the EU in the period 2021–2030 by EUR 350 billion more than in the period 2011–2020, representing an increase of around EUR 90 billion per annum compared to the investments needed to achieve current 2030 climate and energy targets (European Commission, 2020d).

The *Sustainable Europe Investment Plan,* also known as the European Green Deal Investment Plan (European Commission, 2020e) is the main investment pillar of the European Green Deal and identifies the main financial instruments designated to support these objectives, and their respective contributions[2] (Figs. 3.2 and 3.3). A novel element of the Plan is the *Just Transition Mechanism* that addresses the social and economic effects of the transition, focusing on the regions, industries and workers expected to be most affected by the green transition. Operationalising the 'leave no one behind' principle, the Just Transition Mechanism reflects a social dimension of the European Geen Deal and the introduction of protective social policies that had not been considered before (Zimmermann & Gengnagel, 2023). A budget of approximately EUR 55 billion over the period 2021–2027 was planned to be mobilised and channelled through three instruments:

(i) A *new Just Transition Fund* (EUR 19.7 billion from the EU plus EUR 7.3 billion of national co-financing, amounting to a total of EUR 27 billion).

[1] https://commission.europa.eu/strategy-and-policy/priorities-2019-2024/european-green-deal/finance-and-green-deal_en

[2] This includes 30% of the EU's multiannual budget (2021–2028) and the EU's *NextGenerationEU* instrument for recovery from the COVID-19 pandemic; at least 37% of the financing received by the EU Member States under the €672.5 billion Recovery and Resilience Facility; at least *30%* of the European Regional Development Fund allocations received by countries, regions, local governments and cities under the EU Cohesion policy; 37% of the Cohesion Fund; and at least 30% of the InvestEU fund (European Commission, 2020e).

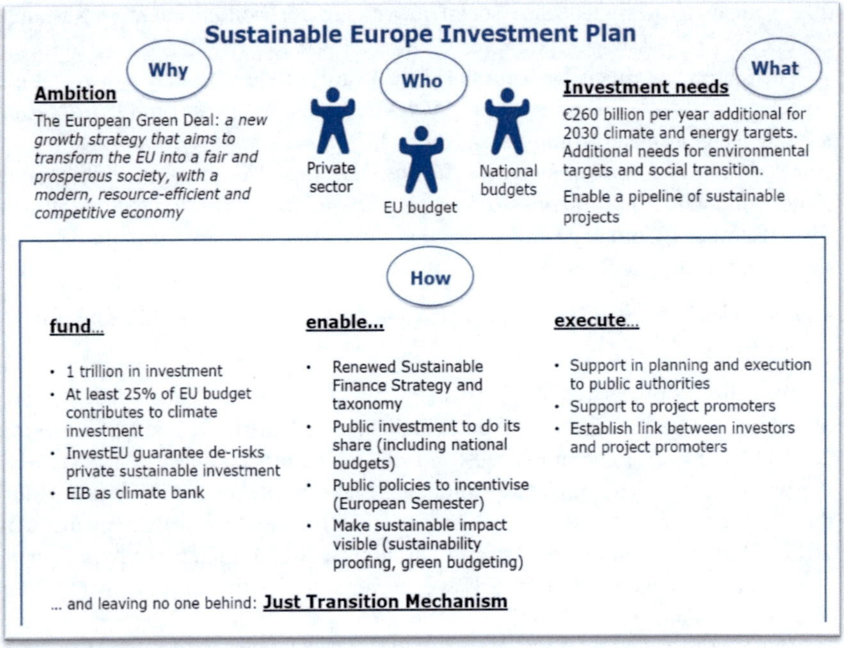

Source: European Commission (2020e)

Fig. 3.2 The Sustainable Europe Investment Plan: key features. Source: European Commission (2020e)

(ii) The *InvestEU 'Just Transition' scheme* as a budgetary guarantee under the InvestEU programme (EUR 10–15 billion in mostly private sector investments).
(iii) A *new Public Sector Loan Facility* (EUR 1.5 billion of grants financed from the EU budget and EUR 10 billion of loans from the European Investment Bank, to mobilise EUR 18.5 billion of public investment).[3]

Complementing the public support, private investments for the green transition were also targeted through innovations in the use of EU financial instruments. For example, the 15-year NextGenerationEU Green Bonds issued in October 2021 raised EUR 12 billion for projects related to energy efficiency, clean energy and climate change adaptation and made the EC the largest bond issuer in the world.[4] Other EU green bonds issued for around USD 300 billion in total are expected over the next five years, turning the EU into the biggest force in the green bond market

[3] https://commission.europa.eu/strategy-and-policy/priorities-2019-2024/european-green-deal/finance-and-green-deal/just-transition-mechanism_en

[4] https://commission.europa.eu/strategy-and-policy/eu-budget/eu-borrower-investor-relations/nextgenerationeu-green-bonds_en

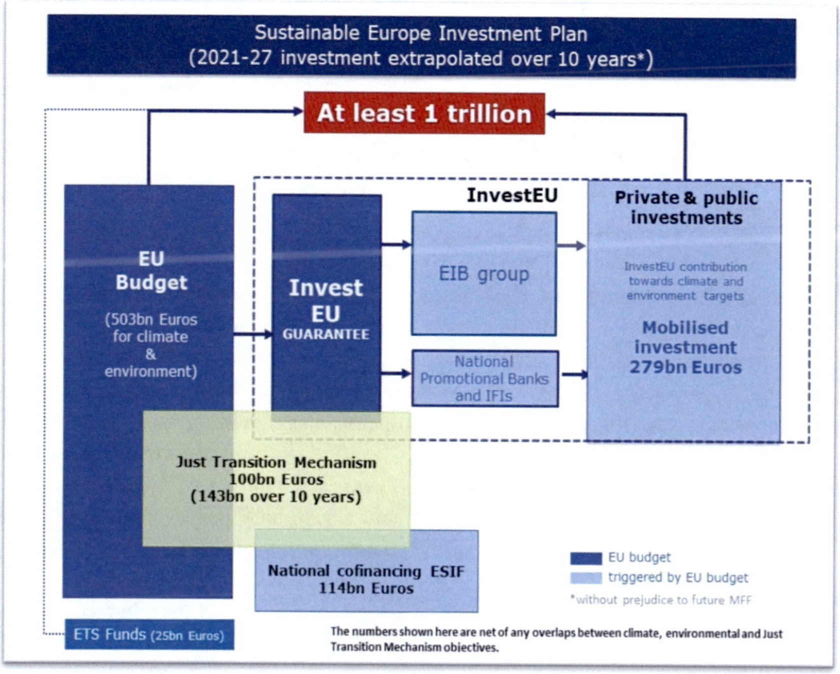

Source: European Commission (2020e)

Fig. 3.3 Financing elements making up at least EUR one trillion over the next decade under the Sustainable Europe Investment Plan. Source: European Commission (2020e)

(Henry & North, 2023). Success on the bond market opened new avenues for the use of these instruments but also highlighted several potentially disruptive issues related to greenwashing, insufficient high-quality green bonds issued relative to market demand and insufficient investment channelled towards projects with substantial climate and environmental impact (European Commission, 2021).

A *Green Public Procurement* was introduced for goods, services and works with a reduced environmental impact throughout their life cycle.[5] The *EU Emissions Trading System (ETS)*—the EU's key tool for reducing greenhouse gas emissions—was reformed in 2022 as part of the 'Fit for 55' package and introduced a new provision to cut emissions 62% by 2030.[6] *The EU Taxonomy Regulation*[7] set out the four conditions that qualify an economic activity as environmentally sustainable and integrates mandatory and voluntary disclosure rules for large financial and non-financial companies as well as financial market participants. This Taxonomy

[5] https://green-business.ec.europa.eu/green-public-procurement_en

[6] https://www.consilium.europa.eu/en/infographics/fit-for-55-eu-emissions-trading-system/

[7] https://finance.ec.europa.eu/sustainable-finance/tools-and-standards/eu-taxonomy-sustainable-activities_en#legislation

approach has been criticised for several limitations in the definition of sectors and the technical screening criteria (Pettingale et al., 2022).

3.2 Reception of the European Green Deal: From 'Paradigm Shift' to 'Colonial Ecology'

With its dual aim to transform the EU's economy *and* society for an enhanced environmental sustainability, the European Green Deal was introduced by the European Commission's President Ursula von der Leyen as *Europe's man on the moon moment* (Hutchinson, 2019). Echoing the sense of ambition, pride and monumental achievement conveyed by Von der Leyen's assertion, other enthusiastic commentators saw the launch of the European Green deal as *'a demonstration of successful European social democracy … a historic breakthrough with its ambitious, challenging, and feasible plan. …a powerful beacon of hope in a world of confusion and instability'* (Sachs, 2019), and a visionary achievement with a deep social impact: *'a new social contract… a unifying force, but above all a clear, concrete, and visionary direction for the European project'* (Tubiana, 2021). Others praised the European Green Deal's global effect: *'a paradigm shift of practical consequence for European—and via an example-setting effect—global sustainability policies'* (Schunz, 2022) and its capacity to offer *'not only an environmental, but also a social and economic opportunity'* (Wolf et al., 2012).

In contrast, critical voices asserted that, far from being an economic paradigm shift, the 'European Green Deal's language *'is full of promise, [but] the strong rhetoric disguises only moderate proposals'* (Friends of the Earth Europe, 2020). Other critical commentators pointed to an *'inherently protectionist, centralised and based on regulatory enforcement'* nature of the European Green Deal, with little attention paid to innovation and potential conflicts over funding (Butler, 2020). Paleari (2022) identified an uneven level of ambition in policy design and implementation, with a stronger focus on the climate and energy policies, and a comparatively lower one in environmental policy, that is not equally equipped in terms of legislative initiatives to deliver on that ambition. On a sharp critical note, Almeida et al. (2023) saw the European Green deal as an instrument that 'reproduces a *colonial and capitalist ecology* by deepening the hegemony of resource imperialism and greening a historically Euro-centred empire' and *'uses a discursive strategy for the "greening" of empire through four registers: (1) making ecological crises profitable opportunities; (2) portraying the EU as "moral" intervener; (3) building on a "green" will to improve; and (4) securitizing and consolidating economic interests'* (p. 2).

Ample reactions and critique have also been expressed in relation to strategies derived from the European Green Deal proposal package that were developed later, for their lack of clarity, detail, vision or depth in governance and implementation. One that triggered much controversy was the *Net Zero Industry Act* that was heavily criticised for failing to provide clear policy objectives and tools (Poitiers et al., 2023) and a clear definition of clean technologies and sectors, favouring larger and richer EU countries through the State aid relaxation proposed (Simon & Taylor, 2023). The Net Zero Industry Act was also criticised for ignoring the circularity dimension and insufficiently representing net-zero industry and trade unions actors in the Net-Zero Europe Platform (European Economic and Social Committee, 2023).

Another example is the *Farm to Fork strategy*, that, after a celebrated launch in May 2020, became the focus of intense controversy a few years later and came to a point where 'many of the most far-reaching reforms are stuck in the mud' following fierce political battles among farmers, EU officials and national diplomats (Wax, 2023). Its provisions for more environmentally friendly farming and healthier diets by the end of the decade sparked significant political tension, to the extent where a document entitled 'Overview of the politically sensitive topics' written by the Commission's Directorate General for Agriculture (DG AGRI) was considered so sensitive that EU officials 'are instructed not to read or carry it in public places, to use encrypted software to save it, and to shred physical copies' (ibid.). The Strategy attracted sharp critique on multiple accounts, e.g. for failing to address the EU's excessive livestock production and over-consumption of meat and dairy, which come at an enormous cost (Hedberg, 2020), for inducing an overall net welfare loss in favour of unverified environmental benefits and costs (Wesseler, 2022) or for failing to create favourable market conditions for innovative technologies and building legitimacy among farmers as the most important user group (Reinhardt, 2023).

To conclude, it is evident that the European Green Deal emerged as a landmark initiative with an ambitious dual aim of transforming the EU's economy and society towards enhanced environmental sustainability. Embraced with enthusiasm and seen as a beacon of hope and a visionary achievement by many, it has not escaped criticism from others. Detractors highlight its perceived moderate proposals, protectionist tendencies and uneven policy implementation and extended their criticism to many specific regulations derived from the initial proposal package of 2019. These mixed reactions reflect the complexity and ambitious scope of the European Green Deal, giving a measure of both its potential and the significant challenges it faces in reshaping Europe's environmental, social and economic landscapes.

References

Almeida, D. V., Kolinjivadi, V., Ferrando, T., Brototi, R., Herrera, H., Vecchione Gonçalves, M., & Van Hecken, G. (2023). The "Greening" of Empire: The European Green Deal as the EU first agenda. *Political Geography, 105*, 102925. https://doi.org/10.1016/j.polgeo.2023.102925

Butler, N. (2020, January 27). *The disruptive effects of Europe's Green Deal*. Financial Times. https://www.ft.com/content/e5c341d2-3c38-11ea-b232-000f4477fbca

European Commission. (2019). COM(2019) 640 final. *The European Green Deal*. https://eur-lex.europa.eu/legal-content/EN/TXT/?uri=COM%3A2019%3A640%3AFIN

European Commission. (2020). COM/2020/788 final. *European Climate Pact*. https://eur-lex.europa.eu/legal-content/EN/TXT/?uri=COM%3A2020%3A788%3AFIN

European Commission. (2020a). *A new industrial strategy for Europe*. COM(2020) 102 final. https://eur-lex.europa.eu/legal-content/EN/TXT/PDF/?uri=CELEX:52020DC0102

European Commission. (2020b). *A new circular economy action plan for a cleaner and more competitive Europe*. COM/2020/98 final. EUR-Lex - 52020DC0098 - EN - EUR-Lex (europa.eu)

European Commission. (2020c). COM(2020) 662 final. *A renovation wave for Europe - greening our buildings, creating jobs, improving lives.* {SWD(2020) 550 final}. https://eur-lex.europa.eu/legal-content/EN/TXT/?qid=1603122220757&uri=CELEX:52020DC0662

European Commission. (2020d). COM(2020) 562 final. *Stepping up Europe's 2030 climate ambition investing in a climate-neutral future for the benefit of our people.* https://eur-lex.europa.eu/legal-content/en/ALL/?uri=CELEX:52020DC0562

European Commission. (2020e). COM/2020/21 final. *Sustainable Europe investment plan European Green Deal investment plan.* https://eur-lex.europa.eu/legal-content/EN/TXT/?uri=CELEX%3A52020DC0021

European Commission. (2021). SWD/2021/181 final. *Impact assessment report accompanying the document proposal for a regulation of the European Parliament and of the Council on European green bonds.* https://eur-lex.europa.eu/legal-content/EN/TXT/?uri=CELEX:52021SC0181

European Economic and Social Committee. (2023). COM(2023) 161 final. Net Zero Industry Act. https://eur-lex.europa.eu/legal-content/EN/ALL/?uri=CELEX:52023AE1157

European Parliament and the Council of the European Union. (2021). *European climate law.* https://eur-lex.europa.eu/legal-content/EN/TXT/?uri=celex%3A32021R1119

Friends of the Earth Europe. (2020, April 30). *Principles for transformation: How the European Green Deal can achieve system change.* https://friendsoftheearth.eu/publication/principles-for-transformation-how-the-european-green-deal-can-achieve-system-change/

Hedberg, A. (2020, May 28). *The farm to fork strategy and the inconvenient truth.* European Policy Centre. https://www.epc.eu/en/publications/The-Farm-to-Fork-Strategy-and-the-inconvenient-truth~33ac84

Henry, P. & North, M. (2023, November 22). What are the green bonds and why is this market growing so fast? *World Economic Forum.* https://www.weforum.org/agenda/2023/11/what-are-green-bonds-climate-change/

Hutchinson, L. (2019, December 11). *'Europe's man on the moon moment': Von der Leyen unveils EU Green Deal.* The Parliament Magazine. https://www.theparliamentmagazine.eu/news/article/europes-man-on-the-moon-moment-von-der-leyen-unveils-eu-green-deal

Mathieu, A. (2021). The European Green Deal – a success story? Nation states must now make the next move. Heinrich Boll Stiftung. May 10. https://www.boell.de/en/2021/05/10/european-green-deal-success-story-nation-states-must-now-make-next-move

Molek-Kozakowska, K. (2023). The hybrid discourse of the 'European Green Deal': Road-mapping economic transition to environmental sustainability (almost) seamlessly. *Critical Discourse Studies, 21*(2), 182–199. https://doi.org/10.1080/17405904.2023.2197607

Monta, M. (2020, May 2020). *The European Green Deal: A game changer or simply a buzzword?*. Friedrich Ebert Stiftung. https://www.researchgate.net/publication/344161380_The_European_Green_Deal_A_game_changer_or_simply_a_buzzword

Oberthür, S., & von Homeyer, I. (2022). From emissions trading to the European Green Deal: The evolution of the climate policy mix and climate policy integration in the EU. *Journal of European Public Policy, 30*(3), 445–468. https://doi.org/10.1080/13501763.2022.2120528

Paleari, S. (2022). The impact of the European Green Deal on EU environmental policy. *The Journal of Environment & Development, 31*(2), 196–220. https://doi.org/10.1177/10704965221082222

Pettingale, H., de Maupeou, S. and Reilly, P. (2022, April 4). EU Taxonomy and the future of reporting. EU Taxonomy and the Future of Reporting (harvard.edu)

Poitiers, N., Sapir, A., Tagliapietra, S., Veugelers, R., & Zettelmeyer, J. (2023, March 9). *The EU net zero industry act and the risk of reviving past failures. How the EU might respond to clean tech subsidies, in the form of a leaked draft law entitled the Net Zero Industry Act (NZIA), is deeply worrisome.* Bruegel. https://www.bruegel.org/first-glance/eu-net-zero-industry-act-and-risk-reviving-past-failures

Reinhardt, T. (2023). The farm to fork strategy and the digital transformation of the agrifood sector—An assessment from the perspective of innovation systems. *Applied Economics perspective and Policy, 45*(2), 819–838. https://doi.org/10.1002/aepp.13246

Sachs, J. D. (2019, December 13). *Europe's Green Deal.* Project Syndicate. https://www.project-syndicate.org/commentary/europe-green-deal-is-global-beacon-by-jeffrey-d-sachs-2019-12.

Schunz, S. (2022). The 'European Green Deal' – A paradigm shift? Transformations in the European Union's sustainability meta-discourse. *Political Research Exchange, 4*(1). https://doi.org/10.1080/2474736X.2022.2085121), https://doi.org/10.1080/2474736X.2022.2085121)

Simon, F. & Taylor, K. (2023, February 2). EU's green industrial plan vague on clean tech, finance, critics say. Euractiv (updated February 3). https://www.euractiv.com/section/energy-environment/news/eus-green-industrial-plan-vague-on-clean-tech-finance-critics-say/

Tubiana, L. (2021). *The Green Deal is the new social contract.* Groupe d'Etudes Géopolitiques. https://geopolitique.eu/en/2021/09/28/laurence-tubiana-green-deal/.

Wax, E. (2023, January 26). *From farm to flop? Political risks choke EU's green food plan.* Politico. https://www.politico.eu/article/blocked-and-delayed-political-risks-choke-eus-green-food-plan-farmers/

Wesseler, J. (2022). The EU's farm-to-fork strategy: An assessment from the perspective of agricultural economics. *Applied Economic Perspectives and Policy, 44*(4), 1826–1843. https://doi.org/10.1002/aepp.13239

Wolf, S., Teitge, J., Mielke, J., et al. (2012). The European Green Deal — More than climate neutrality. *Intereconomics, 56*, 99–107. https://doi.org/10.1007/s10272-021-0963-z

Zimmermann, K., & Gengnagel, V. (2023). Mapping the social dimension of the European Green Deal. *European Journal of Social Security, 25*(4), 523–544. https://doi.org/10.1177/13882627231208698

Part II
European Green Deal's impact on the EU Single Market

Chapter 4
The EU Single Market: Key Features and Links with the European Green Deal

Abstract The European Green Deal has seen the Single Market from the onset as a driver for the twin green and digital transitions. Numerous strategies and regulatory initiatives that have operationalised the European Green Deal since its launch in December 2019 included specific references to the Single Market, aiming for broad-ranging impacts. Evidence of impact to date indicate notable changes within the Single Market in several areas. Many of these changes are a result of research and innovation projects.

4.1 The EU Single Market: Key Features

A cornerstone of the EU's economic and political project and European integration, the Single Market, also known as the European internal market, represents a unified and borderless economic area comprising the 27 EU Member States, as well as Iceland, Liechtenstein and Norway (through the Agreement on the European Economic Area) and Switzerland (partial access through bilateral agreements). It guarantees the free movement of goods, capital, services and people, known as the 'four freedoms' that are embedded in the EU's treaties as the basis of the Single Market legislative framework.

Achieving the four freedoms within a common market and customs union was a core objective of the European Economic Community (EEC), the precursor of the EU, since its establishment in 1957. Implementing this objective, however, was a difficult process due to numerous technical, regulatory, legal and bureaucratic obstacles to the integration of the four freedoms, political crises and border management issues, diverging economic interests leading to protectionist measures in many of the Member States.

The European Parliament played a significant role during its first decade as a directly elected political institution (1979–1989) in consolidating the EEC internal market (Warlouzet, 2020). It had a significant influence on the European Commission that, under its new President, Jacques Delors, launched in 1985 the paper *Completing the Internal Market: White Paper from the Commission to the European Council*—an ambitious programme to complete the Single Market by

M. Ranga, *Single Market 2.0*, Contributions to Economics,
https://doi.org/10.1007/978-3-031-83220-8_4

1992 (Commission of the European Communities, 1985). This process was consolidated one year later, in 1986, by the adoption of the Single European Act (SEA) that entered into force on 1 July 1987. The SEA set the deadline of 31 December 1992 for the completion of the internal market and introduced a new framework and cooperation mechanisms to dismantle trade barriers and consolidate the four freedoms. It enhanced decision-making mechanisms by introducing qualified majority voting for areas such as common customs tariffs, the freedom to provide services, the free movement of capital and the harmonisation of national legislation. By the end of this period, over 90% of the legislative acts foreseen in the 1985 White Paper had been adopted, primarily using the qualified majority voting rule.[1]

A few years later, in 1992, the Maastricht Treaty formally established the EU and laid the groundwork for the Economic and Monetary Union and a single currency—the Euro—paving the way for the launch of the Single Market on 1 January 1993. The Single Market continued to get new strengths in the following years through the provisions of several key EU documents. The Lisbon Strategy (2000) acknowledged that *"Rapid work is required in order to complete the internal market in certain sectors and to improve under-performance in others in order to ensure the interests of business and consumers"*[2] and asked the Commission, the Council and the Member States to put in place a broad package of economic reforms for a complete and fully operational internal market. The Services Directive (2006)[3] created a legal framework for a more open and competitive market for services within the EU, ensuring the freedom of establishment and the free movement of services between the Member States and simplifying the process for service providers to operate across EU borders. The Treaty of Lisbon[4] (2007) reinforced the legal and institutional framework of the Single Market, clarifying the EU's competences in various policy areas: exclusive (e.g. on the customs union, on the competition rules for the internal market, the monetary policy for the Member States with the euro currency, etc.) or shared with the Member States (e.g. on the internal market).

The Single Market Act, in its two parts—Single Market Act I (European Commission, 2011) and Single Market Act II (European Commission, 2012)—introduced several levers to stimulate the growth of the Single Market.[5] These were

---

[1] https://www.europarl.europa.eu/factsheets/en/sheet/33/the-internal-market-general-principles

[2] https://www.europarl.europa.eu/summits/lis1_en.htm

[3] Directive 2006/123/EC of the European Parliament and of the Council of 12 December 2006 on services in the internal market. https://eur-lex.europa.eu/legal-content/EN/TXT/?uri=celex%3A32006L0123

[4] Treaty of Lisbon amending the Treaty on European Union and the Treaty establishing the European Community, signed at Lisbon, 13 December 2007. https://eur-lex.europa.eu/legal-content/EN/TXT/?uri=celex%3A12007L%2FTXT

[5] The Single Market Act I introduced 12 levers to boost growth and strengthen confidence in the economy: (1) access to finance for SMEs, (2) mobility for citizens, (3) intellectual property rights, (4) consumer empowerment, (5) services, (6) networks, (7) digital single market, (8) social entrepreneurship, (9) taxation, (10) social cohesion, (11) business environment and (12) public procurement. The Single Market Act II complemented that with a second set of four levers to further

followed in 2015 by two other important initiatives for the Single Market consolidation: the launch of the Capital Markets Union (CMU),[6] creating a single market for capital by removing barriers to cross-border investment and lowering costs of funding within the EU, and the Digital Single Market strategy,[7] aiming to stimulate the digital economy and ensure better access for consumers and businesses to online goods and services across Europe. Both these initiatives have seen a significant boost since 2020 from the European Green Deal that considers the Single Market as key to the green and digital transitions (e.g. the Digital Services Act aims to create a safer digital space for users and companies and the Digital Markets Act to guarantee a competitive and fair digital sector, both adopted in 2022). In April 2021, the Single Market Programme was presented as the main operational framework for the period 2021–2027 with a budget of EUR 4.2 billion.[8,9]

The implementation of the four freedoms within the Single Market set in motion a process of harmonising regulations and standards and creating a level playing field for businesses operating in the EU that increased EU integration and generated a wide range of benefits. Exports of both goods and services within and outside the EU boosted SMEs' internationalisation and competitiveness and further increased contributions to international value chains. According to the 2020 Eurobarometer on SMEs, start-ups, scale-ups and entrepreneurship, 23% of all EU SMEs exported to countries within the Single Market, 9% exported to European countries outside the EU, and 4% exported to North America (European Commission, 2023, p. 11). From 1992 to 2008, the Single Market has generated an extra 2.77 million jobs in the EU and an additional 2.13% in GDP (European Commission, 2012) due to the recognition of professional qualifications across the Single Market and removal of work visas. Free travel in the EU and possibility for EU citizens to work, live and retire in the EU, as well as possibility for young people to study abroad, created new opportunities on the labour and education markets. More choices for energy, health and banking services and safer products and services have become available for EU citizens through common high standards within the Single Market, as well as more possibilities for EU social security, consumer rights, health and safety and cashless euro payments within the EU and associated countries. Recent changes to European regulations, such as the European company law that facilitates the establishment and operations of companies in the EU and adds new digital facilities for cross-border

develop the Single Market: (1) developing fully integrated networks in the Single Market, (2) fostering mobility of citizens and businesses across borders, (3) supporting the digital economy across Europe and (4) strengthening social entrepreneurship, cohesion and consumer confidence.

[6] https://finance.ec.europa.eu/capital-markets-union-and-financial-markets/capital-markets-union/what-capital-markets-union_en

[7] https://eur-lex.europa.eu/summary/chapter/31.html

[8] https://commission.europa.eu/funding-tenders/find-funding/eu-funding-programmes/single-market-programme/overview_en

[9] https://commission.europa.eu/strategy-and-policy/eu-budget/performance-and-reporting/programme-performance-statements/single-market-programme-performance_en

operations through the Business Registers Interconnection System (BRIS), contributed to further integration.

Estimates of EU membership impact on economic growth and productivity found generally positive and large effects, with considerable heterogeneity across countries, despite a recognised difficulty to perform robust econometric determinations.[10] Estimates of EU membership identified an increase in the EU GDP by 8–9% on average over the last 30 years due to the Single Market's boost of intra-EU trade flows through elimination of trade tariffs and reduction in non-tariff barriers, while the opening up of domestic economies led to increased competition and lowered prices (In't Veld, 2019). Similar positive effects were reported in the literature (e.g. Badinger, 2005; Crespo Cuaresma et al., 2008; Campos et al., 2019) and are more visible in Central and Eastern Europe and smaller EU Member States (Matkowski & Próchniak, 2014; Lehtimäki & Sondermann, 2020).

In 2023, at the 30th anniversary of the Single Market, a broad range of integration advancements and benefits were reported[11] but also several challenges to a complete integration (European Commission, 2023), as presented in Box 4.1.

Box 4.1 Challenges to the Single Market Integration

- "In some areas for instance, there is no truly integrated European market as missing legislation, administrative obstacles, and a lack of enforcement leaves the full potential of the single market unexploited. Confidence in the single market also needs boosting to help stimulate economic growth" (European Commission, https://single-market-economy.ec.europa.eu/single-market/single-market-act_en).
- "…the EU's single market is far weaker than assumed and not nearly as 'single' as the name suggests. It is full of shortcomings and contains hundreds of barriers and distortions that seriously and detrimentally impact the EU's ability to stimulate and encourage investment. This must be addressed by EU policymakers as a matter of urgency" (Pelkmans, 2024).
- "…the single market remains far from complete. While many physical goods — cars, say — largely trade frictionlessly in a homogeneous

(continued)

[10] Such determinations involve a multitude of factors that can be hard to capture, such as heterogeneity of country experiences before and after their EU accession, particularities of 'deep' versus 'shallow' integration (Lawrence, 2000), specific conditions at the time of successive EU enlargements, effects in different areas, such as goods, finance, services, technology, policies, differences in the institutional and regulatory changes required for accession in various countries, etc.

[11] Trade integration in goods for the 12 Member States of the Single Market increased from 11% in 1993 to 23% in 2021 for today's EU-27, while trade integration in services increased from 3% to 6% in the same period. Potential benefits of removing obstacles to free intra-EU services are estimated at between €279 billion (when the gap with the Member States performers that are performing best in terms of obstacles is reduced by 50%) and €457 billion (if the gap is reduced by 80%) of additional GDP per year in the long term (European Commission, 2023, pp. 5–9).

Box 4.1 (continued)

EU-wide economy, national borders still matter a lot, especially in services. [...] The fragmentation of banking as well as capital funding makes a mockery of the free flow of capital. This is the challenge that the projects of the Banking Union and Capital Markets Union are supposed to address but so far have not. The single market is also incomplete in its political functions. It has now become commonplace to talk of a 'Brussels effect' by which non-EU companies voluntarily adopt EU standards." (Sandbu, 2024).

- "Despite ambitions for a more integrated Europe, progress has been limited, with the Single Market far from complete. National political and protectionist tendencies often prioritise individual state interests over collective European goals, obstructing the vision of a seamless economic area allowing free movement of goods, services, people, and capital. [...] Rising nationalism and shifts towards 'Strategic Autonomy' in the EU have stalled essential market reforms and fostered protectionist policies, undermining global trade norms and the liberalisation progress achieved in the past decades. If the European Parliament shifts further towards national-populist representation following the 2024 elections, these inward-oriented, protectionist tendencies could be exacerbated. To counteract such developments and achieve a truly unified market, the EU needs a deep re-evaluation of its integration strategies, addressing legal fragmentation and cultural barriers through substantial reforms" (Bauer et al., 2024).

Source: own selection

In a comprehensive inventory of barriers to proper functioning of the Single Market and the EU economy, the European Commission identified 31 horizontal and 52 sector-specific barriers that were confirmed by the business community (European Commission, 2020). Some of these barriers pertain to EU policy, but many others relate to national regulation, administrative and business practices.[12] Findings show that some important markets, such as those for financial services, energy and transport, are still predominantly national, with e-commerce rules, standards and practices that vary significantly between the EU Member States. These barriers have been a constant preoccupation for the European Commission's Directorate-General for Internal Market, Industry, Entrepreneurship and SMEs (DG GROW), which reported in the 2024 edition of the *Annual Single Market*

[12] National barriers include a lack of information and complex procedures; national requirements in services; administrative requirements for posting workers, taxation and goods issues (e.g. labelling requirements, problems with mutual recognition), as well as broader issues such as transport bottlenecks and a lack of skilled workers and mobility (European Commission, 2023, p. 10).

Table 4.1 A functioning Single Market

KPI	Description	Target	Latest EU value
KPI 1: Integration in the Single Market	Integration in the Single Market: trade over GDP	Up	26.3% for goods (2022) 23.5% for goods (2021) 7.5% for services (2022) 6.6% for services (2021)
KPI 2: Conformity deficit (incorrectly transposed directives)	It measures the number of directives transposed for which infringement proceedings for incorrect transposition have been launched by the Commission	0.5%	1.2% (2023) 1.3% (2022)

Source: European Commission (2024)

Report (European Commission, 2024) an increased integration for goods and services and a reduction in the conformity deficit from 2022 to 2023 (Table 4.1).

Progress in market integration often came at the expense of more flexibility in the implementation of laws that govern the Single Market, such as the EU competition policy (Howarth & Sadeh, 2010; Raudla & Spendzharova, 2022). Also, successive crises (e.g. the European debt crisis of 2009–2010, Brexit, the recent COVID-19 pandemic, etc) presented distinct challenges to European integration and tested the resilience of the EU, often imposing course adjustments that some called *"a shift from market integration to the integration of core state powers"* (Genschel & Jachtenfuchs, 2018). At the same time, several reforms adopted along the way strengthened the EU's authority through a process of "failing forward" (Jones et al., 2021) and "integration through crisis" (Biermann et al., 2019).

4.2 Links Between the European Green Deal and the Single Market

The European Green Deal has seen the Single Market as a driving force for the green and digital transition and aimed to transform it into a more sustainable and competitive economic area. The main channel for this transformation was a comprehensive regulatory framework for the Single Market that was embedded in the initial

European Green Deal proposal package launched in December 2019 (European Commission, 2019).[13]

This wide range of policies designed to integrate environmental sustainability into all the economic sectors of the EU have been operationalised in several key documents that followed later, to ensure the implementation of the European Green Deal:

- *The Sustainable Europe Investment Plan* (also known as the European Green Deal Investment Plan) (European Commission, 2020a) mobilised significant public and private investment towards sustainable projects. The Plan defined three dimensions for the Single Market's role in enabling the green transition: (i) mobilisation of at least EUR 1 trillion of sustainable investments for climate and environment over the next decade from the EU budget and private funding; (ii) creation of a framework for private investors and the public sector, providing the tools to identify sustainable investments; and (iii) support to public administrations and project promoters in identifying, structuring and executing sustainable projects. Also, the Just Transition Mechanism, as part of the Plan, sought to facilitate the green transition by supporting regions and sectors most affected by the transition away from fossil fuels.
- *The New Industrial Strategy for Europe* of March 2020 (European Commission, 2020b) and its update of May 2021 (European Commission, 2021) focused on the EU industry's global competitiveness and strategic autonomy and sought to reduce dependencies on non-EU countries for critical raw materials, technologies and products while securing supply chains and critical infrastructures within the Single Market. Several measures were dedicated to SMEs, to increase resilience, combat late payments and support solvency. To promote the green transition, the strategy encouraged the adoption of renewable energy, energy efficiency and circular economy principles across industries. For the digital transition, investments in digital infrastructure, skills and technologies were prioritised within the Single Market, including the development of data spaces, AI, cybersecurity and 5G networks. To create a conducive environment for innovation and technological advancements, R&D investments were planned across various sectors, as well as financial support and resources for SMEs to innovate and scale operations within the Single Market. The strategy laid the foundation for several industrial alliances at EU level, in key areas such as batteries, hydrogen and cloud computing, to pool resources and expertise and position the EU as a global leader in sustainable and competitive industrial practices.

[13]Most of these provisions are included in the section on 'Mobilising Industry for a Clean and Circular Economy', for example, expansion of low-emission technologies, sustainable products, services and jobs; decarbonisation and modernisation of energy-intensive industries; introduction of new legislation and more sustainable product policies; as well as new policies for access to critical resources for clean technologies, digital, space and defence applications.

- *The Circular Economy Action Plan* (European Commission, 2020c) aimed to modernise the EU economy and the Single Market by fostering sustainable product design, reducing waste and promoting resource efficiency. The Action Plan impacted various industries within the Single Market by mandating new standards for product life cycle management and waste reduction, promoting circularity in production and consumption in key product value chains, ensuring regulatory coherence and market integration and fostering business creation and entrepreneurship.
- *The Green Deal Industrial Plan for the Net-Zero Age* (European Commission, 2023a) put Europe's net-zero industry in the lead. The four pillars of the Plan have significant implications for the Single Market by supporting (i) a predictable and simplified regulatory environment with uniform standards across EU Member States to reduce trade barriers within the Single Market and facilitate the free movement of goods and services, (ii) faster access to funding for clean-tech production in Europe, (ii) skilled workforce for the net-zero industry and (iv) open trade and international cooperation to support the green transition and protect the EU market from unfair trade practices. The Plan also introduced measures to streamline administrative processes and speed up procedures for green projects, reduce the bureaucratic burden on businesses and encourage faster deployment of clean technologies.
- Energy policies such as the *Renovation Wave* (European Commission, 2020d) and the *revised Renewable Energy Directive*[14] that sets an overall renewable energy target of at least 42.5% binding at EU level by 2030—but aiming for 45%—encouraged energy efficiency and the adoption of renewable energy sources across the EU.

All these documents opened multiple directions for the European Green Deal impact on the Single Market. A key question now is how effective have these strategies been? Evidence on the actual progress in reaching these objectives is still relatively limited, as impact data have only started to emerge in the last few years. The 2023 and 2024 editions of the Annual Single Market Reports prepared by the European Commission's Directorate General for the Internal Market, Industry, Entrepreneurship and SMEs (DG GROW) provide some relevant insights (European Commission, 2023a and 2024, respectively).

For instance, the 2024 Annual Single Market Report highlights several regulatory acts that have been adopted to develop the Digital Markets within the Single Market, creating a uniform set of rules for businesses to operate across the EU (e.g. the Digital Services Act, the Data Governance Act, the Data Act and the AI Act). The *SME Relief Package*[15] was adopted in September 2023 to support SMEs' competitiveness and growth, especially for the so-called small mid-cap enterprises (SMCs)

---

[14] https://eur-lex.europa.eu/legal-content/EN/TXT/?uri=CELEX%3A32023L2413&qid=1699364355105

[15] https://single-market-economy.ec.europa.eu/news/unleashing-potential-europes-small-businesses-2023-09-28_en

that are prominent in key industrial ecosystems for the green and digital transition, such as electronics, aerospace and defence, energy, energy-intensive industries and health. Instruments such as the *Net-Zero Industry Act*, the *Chips Act* and the *Critical Raw Materials Act* provided significant investment to strengthen the EU's domestic manufacturing capacity. The *Industrial Alliances*[16] established since 2017 in several sectors related to the green and digital transition fostered cooperation along supply chains in key technologies. The seven *Important Projects of Common European Interest (IPCEIs)*[17] approved to date mobilised EUR 27.9 billion of national public support and more than EUR 50 billion of private investments to support breakthrough innovations or infrastructure projects in critical technologies areas. The *Innovation Fund*,[18] financed through the revenues of the EU Emissions Trading System, has supported innovation in net-zero technologies towards full technological and commercial maturity and has become a key public instrument to deploy the EU green deal industrial strategy. Finally, the *Strategic Technologies for Europe Platform (STEP)*[19] was launched in August 2024 to support critical technologies in Europe in three target investment areas: digital technologies and deep-tech innovation, clean and resource efficient technologies and Biotechnologies, as well as the development of skills necessary to those critical technologies.

European Green Deal effects on the EU industrial and competitiveness policies have also been analysed in recent works by academic researchers and policy analysts. Veugelers et al. (2024) identify the concept of 'green industrial policy' as a next development stage in the historical evolution of the European industrial policy under the European Green Deal, combining the elements environmental sustainability and economic growth, under the imperative to transition towards carbon neutrality. Renda (2024) questions the capacity of the EU's industrial policy to solve Europe's 'trilemma' of boosting competitiveness, economic security and strategic autonomy while also ensuring progress towards decarbonisation. Lausberg et al. (2023) call for a reform of the EU regulatory framework to address Europe's decrease in competitiveness that resulted from the advancement of its green and digital transitions. Radosevic (2024) identifies an ample transition of the Single Market from a rules-based open market to a multidimensional mechanism focused on promoting green growth locally and globally that changes rationales, allocation directionality, governance, relationship to global markets and metrics.

The review of changes driven by the European Green Deal within the Single Market shows that many of them are a result of research and innovation projects. That doesn't come as a surprise, considering that innovation is widely acknowledged as an enabler of competitiveness and environmental sustainability. However, the synergies between industrial, competitiveness and innovation policies and their

[16]https://single-market-economy.ec.europa.eu/industry/industrial-alliances_en

[17]https://competition-policy.ec.europa.eu/state-aid/ipcei_en

[18]https://climate.ec.europa.eu/eu-action/eu-funding-climate-action/innovation-fund_en

[19]https://strategic-technologies.europa.eu/index_en

mutually reinforcing effects claimed in many policy documents remain largely unexplored, as we discuss in the next chapter.

References

Badinger, H. (2005). Growth effects of economic integration: Evidence from the EU member states. *Review of World Economics, 141*(1), 50–78. https://doi.org/10.1007/s10290-005-0015-y

Bauer, M., Pandya, D., Sharma, V., & Sisto, E. (2024, June 2024). *Reinventing Europe's single market: A way forward to align ideals and action*. European Centre for International Political Economy. https://ecipe.org/publications/reinventing-europes-single-market-align-ideals-and-action/

Biermann, F., Guérin, N., Jagdhuber, S., Rittberger, B., & Weiss, M. (2019). Political (non) reform in the euro crisis and the refugee crisis: A liberal intergovernmentalist explanation. *Journal of European Public Policy, 26*(2), 246–266. https://doi.org/10.1080/13501763.2017.1408670

Campos, N. F., Coricelli, F., & Moretti, L. (2019). Institutional integration and economic growth in Europe. *Journal of Monetary Economics, 103*, 88–104. https://doi.org/10.1016/j.jmoneco.2018.08.001

Commission of the European Communities. (1985, June). *Completing the internal market: White paper from the Commission to the European Council.* https://europa.eu/documents/comm/white_papers/pdf/com1985_0310_f_en.pdf

Crespo Cuaresma, J., Ritzberger-Grünwald, D., & Silgoner, M. A. (2008). Growth, convergence and EU membership. *Applied Economics, 40*(5), 643–656. https://doi.org/10.1080/00036840600749524

European Commission. (2011). COM/2011/0206 final. *Single market act twelve levers to boost growth and strengthen confidence "Working together to create new growth"*. EUR-Lex - 52011DC0206 - EN - EUR-Lex (europa.eu).

European Commission. (2012). COM/2012/0573 final. *Single market act II Together for new growth.* https://eur-lex.europa.eu/legal-content/EN/TXT/?uri=celex:52012DC0573.

European Commission. (2019). COM/2019/640 final. *The European Green Deal.* https://eur-lex.europa.eu/legal-content/EN/TXT/?uri=COM%3A2019%3A640%3AFIN

European Commission. (2020). SWD(2020) 54 final. *Business journey on the single market: Practical obstacles and barriers*. https://eur-lex.europa.eu/legal-content/EN/TXT/?uri=CELEX%3A52020SC0054

European Commission. (2020a). COM(2020) 21 final. *Sustainable Europe Investment Plan European Green Deal Investment Plan.* https://eur-lex.europa.eu/legal-content/EN/TXT/?uri=CELEX%3A52020DC0021

European Commission. (2020b). COM(2020) 102 final. *A new industrial strategy for Europe.* https://eur-lex.europa.eu/legal-content/EN/TXT/?uri=CELEX:52020DC0102

European Commission. (2020c). COM(2020) 98 final. *A new circular economy action plan. For a cleaner and more competitive Europe.* https://eur-lex.europa.eu/legal-content/EN/TXT/?uri=COM%3A2020%3A98%3AFIN

European Commission. (2020d). COM(2020) 662 final. *A renovation wave for Europe - greening our buildings, creating jobs, improving lives.* https://eur-lex.europa.eu/legal-content/EN/TXT/?qid=1603122220757&uri=CELEX:52020DC0662

European Commission. (2021). COM(2021) 350 final. *Annual single market report 2021 Updating the 2020 new industrial strategy: Building a stronger single market for Europe's recovery.* https://commission.europa.eu/document/download/9ab0244c-6ca3-4b11-bef9-422c7eb34f39_en?filename=communication-industrial-strategy-update-2020_en.pdf

European Commission. (2023). SWD(2023) 26 final. *2023 Annual single market report: Single market at 30*, pp. 5–9. https://single-market-economy.ec.europa.eu/system/files/2023-01/ASMR 2023.pdf

European Commission. (2023a). COM/2023/62 final. *A Green Deal industrial plan for the net-zero age.* https://eur-lex.europa.eu/legal content/EN/TXT/?uri=CELEX%3A52023DC0062

European Commission. (2024). COM(2024) 77 final. *The 2024 annual single market and competitiveness report.* https://eur-lex.europa.eu/legal-content/EN/TXT/?uri=CELEX%3A52024DC0077

Genschel, P., & Jachtenfuchs, M. (2018). From market integration to core state powers: The Eurozone crisis, the refugee crisis and integration theory. *Journal of Common Market Studies, 56*, 178–196. https://doi.org/10.1111/jcms.12654

Howarth, D., & Sadeh, T. (2010). The ever-incomplete single market: Differentiation and the evolving frontier of integration. *Journal of European Public Policy, 17*(7), 922–935. https://doi.org/10.1080/13501763.2010.499220

In't Veld, J. (2019, February). *Quantifying the economic effects of the single market in a structural macromodel.* Discussion paper 094. European Commission. https://economy-finance.ec.europa.eu/system/files/2019-02/dp094_en.pdf

Jones, E., Kelemen, R. D., & Meunier, S. (2021). Failing forward? Crises and patterns of European integration. *Journal of European Public Policy, 28*(10), 1519–1536. https://doi.org/10.1080/13501763.2021.1954068

Lausberg, P., Otero-Iglesias, M., Riekeles, G., & González-Agotel, A. (2023, April 17). *Towards a competitive edge: Reforming the EU regulatory framework.* Discussion Paper. European Policy Centre. https://www.epc.eu/content/Regulatory_DP_v3.pdf

Lawrence, R. Z. (2000). *Regionalism, multilateralism, and deeper integration.* Brookings Institution Press. https://www.brookings.edu/books/regionalism-multinationalism-and-deeper-integration/

Lehtimäki, J. & Sondermann, D. (2020). *Baldwin vs. Cecchini revisited: the growth impact of the European Single Market*, European Central Bank Working Paper Series, No 2392/April 2020. https://www.ecb.europa.eu/pub/pdf/scpwps/ecb.wp2392~83000b6b14.en.pdf

Matkowski, Z., & Próchniak, M. (2014). Economic convergence between the CEE-8 and the European Union. *Eastern European Economics, 45*(1), 59–76. https://doi.org/10.2753/EEE0012-8775450103

Pelkmans, J. (2024, February 5). *For the EU's prosperity, we must empower the single market now.* CEPS commentary. https://www.ceps.eu/for-the-eus-prosperity-we-must-empower-the-single-market-now/

Radosevic, S. (2024, February 23). *EU single market embracing 'green' industrial policy: paradigm shift and challenges.* DG GROW Single Market Economics Briefs. https://single-market-economy.ec.europa.eu/publications/eu-single-market-embracing-green-industrial-policy-paradigm-shift-and-challenges_en

Raudla, R., & Spendzharova, A. (2022). Challenges to the European single market at thirty: Renationalisation, resilience, or renewed integration? *Journal of European Integration, 44*(1), 1–17. https://doi.org/10.1080/07036337.2021.2011263

Renda, A. (2024, April). *What North Star for future EU industrial policy? CEPS In-Depth Analysis.* https://cdn.ceps.eu/wp-content/uploads/2024/04/CEPS-InDepthAnalysis-2024-07_EU-North-Star-for-EU-Industrial-Policy-3.pdf

Sandbu, M. (2024, February 8). *The strategic crossroads for the EU's single market.* Financial Times. https://www.ft.com/content/13d6ca67-eebb-4ea7-939b-1d03fec68b81

Veugelers, R., Tagliapietra, S., & Trasi, C. (2024). Green industrial policy in Europe: Past, present, and prospects. *Journal of Industry, Competition and Trade, 24*, 4. Published online: 14 March 2024. https://doi.org/10.1007/s10842-024-00418-5

Warlouzet, L. (2020). *Completing the single market: The European Parliament and economic integration, 1979–1989.* European Parliament History Series Study. https://www.europarl.europa.eu/RegData/etudes/STUD/2020/646120/EPRS_STU(2020)646120_EN.pdf

Chapter 5
The EU Single Market from an 'Innovation System' Perspective: An Analytical Framework

Abstract Research and innovation have been acknowledged as one of the nine interlinked and mutually reinforcing drivers of Single Market's sustainable competitiveness. Specific KPIs have been introduced to assess progress, but they have some limitations both in number and in scope. To better capture the impact of the European Green Deal, we propose an 'innovation system' perspective of the EU Single Market, centred on its quintessential structural element—the industrial ecosystem. The industrial ecosystems are themselves a set of interconnected sectoral and technological innovation systems that can be analysed using the seven functions of an innovation system as an exploratory tool.

As detailed in Chap. 4, the European Green Deal has a strong emphasis on innovation. That was evident from the initial proposal package launched in December 2019 and was extended through the various strategies, directives and initiatives introduced in the following years. The *New Industrial Strategy for Europe* (European Commission, 2020) explicitly expresses in its Sect. 3.5 the deep connections between industrial strategy and innovation for the successful implementation of the European Green Deal as Europe's new growth strategy: *'If Europe wants to lead the twin transitions, the industrial strategy has to be an industrial innovation strategy at heart'*. This principle is reflected in a myriad of measures introduced both in this strategy and subsequent ones, reflecting the commitment to integrating innovation into the core of Europe's growth strategy.

The recent communication *Long-Term Competitiveness of the EU: Looking Beyond 2030* (European Commission, 2023) identifies research and innovation as one of the nine interlinked and mutually reinforcing drivers of Single Market's competitiveness (Fig. 5.1) and provides specific KPIs for assessing progress that are presented on an annual basis in the Single Market and Competitiveness Scoreboard. However, as Renda (2024) remarks, most of the drivers reflect inputs rather than outputs or outcomes: 'the eight drivers of sustainable competitiveness encompass mostly input indicators, rather than outputs or outcomes. Importantly, the completion and effective functioning of the single market is listed as driver, which confirms the intermediate nature of the single market as a goal … Among the "evergreens", the drivers include spending on research, development and innovation

M. Ranga, *Single Market 2.0*, Contributions to Economics,
https://doi.org/10.1007/978-3-031-83220-8_5

Fig. 5.1 The nine mutually reinforcing drivers of Europe's competitiveness. Source: European Commission (2023)

Table 5.1 KPIs related to research and innovation as a driver for Single Market's competitiveness

KPI	Description	Target	Latest EU value
KPI 6: R&D expenditure as a percentage of GDP	The total R&D expenditure (public and private)	>3% beyond 2030	2.2% (2021) 2.3% (2020)
KPI 7: Number of patent applications per million inhabitants	Patents reflect the capacity of an economy to exploit knowledge and indicate the competitiveness edge that can be obtained through innovation	Up	EPO-EU 151.1 (2022) 151.75 (2021)

Source: European Commission (2024), section 4.

as a share of GDP, accompanied by public mission-oriented investment, which is interpreted as based on input rather than assessed on its actual output, outcome or impact' (p. 7).

The output or outcome indicators for research and innovation as a driver of the Single Market's sustainable competitiveness are indeed limited, both in number and in scope. The Annual Single Market Report 2024 (European Commission, 2024) provides two KPIs for research and innovation (Table 5.1):

- KPI 6—R&D expenditure as a percentage of GDP
- KPI 7—number of patent applications per million inhabitants

KPI 7 is just one of the four indicators of the composite Innovation Output Indicator (IOI) developed by the European Commission in 2013 and published periodically ever since.[1] They measure the extent to which ideas from innovative sectors can reach the market, providing better jobs and making Europe more competitive. The IOI complements KPI 6—R&D expenditure as a percentage of GDP (R&D intensity)—as well as other indicators of the Commission, included in the Innovation Union Scoreboard (IUS) and the Summary Innovation Index (SII).

The two KPIs provide a measure of the Single Market's innovation performance at the level of the EU Member States, identifying leaders and laggards. However, there are some limitations arising from several factors. On the one hand, KPI 6 is influenced by industry structure of each country (Mathieu & van Pottelsberghe de la Potterie, 2010; Reinstaller & Unterlass, 2012, cited in Janger et al., 2017), favouring countries with R&D-intensive industries, and may include also unproductive R&D investment. On the other hand, KPI 7, as part of the IOI, reasonably reflects processes of structural change but does not appropriately address structural upgrading, thus overrating countries specialised in knowledge-intensive sectors far from the technological frontier and underrating countries specialised in less knowledge-intensive sectors close to the frontier (Janger et al., 2017).

To better capture the innovation impact of the European Green Deal on the Single Market, we propose an in-depth exploration of the EU Single Market from an 'innovation system' perspective. The analysis is centred on the quintessential structural element of the Single Market—the industrial ecosystem.

The 'industrial ecosystem' concept was introduced in the *New Industrial Strategy for Europe* (European Commission, 2020) as part of the new vision of EU industrial strategy associated with the twin green and digital transition. The new vision was more entrepreneurial and more innovation- and technologically oriented and recognised the need to design and co-create solutions by industry with a broad range of stakeholders. In this document, the Commission pledges to 'undertake a thorough screening and analysis of industrial needs and identify ecosystems needing a tailor-made approach' (p. 16).

Building on the principles of industrial ecology (Lowe & Evans, 1995; Korhonen, 2001; Adner, 2017; Autio et al., 2018), the 'industrial ecosystem' concept started to take shape in the *first Annual Single Market Repor*t (European Commission, 2021). The report employs it to capture the effects of the uneven economic contraction across economic sectors caused by the COVID-19 pandemic and to explore interdependencies between different economic actors. To that end, the report identifies

[1] The four components are (i) technological innovation as measured by patent applications; (ii) employment in knowledge-intensive activities as a percentage of total employment; (iii) competitiveness of knowledge-intensive goods and services, based on both the contribution of the trade balance of high-tech and medium-tech products to the total trade balance and the knowledge-intensive services as a share of the total services exports; and (iv) employment in fast-growing firms of innovative sectors. The four indicators have been chosen for their policy relevance, data quality, international availability, cross-country comparability and robustness. Source: https://ec.europa.eu/eurostat/statistics-explained/SEPDF/cache/49225.pdf

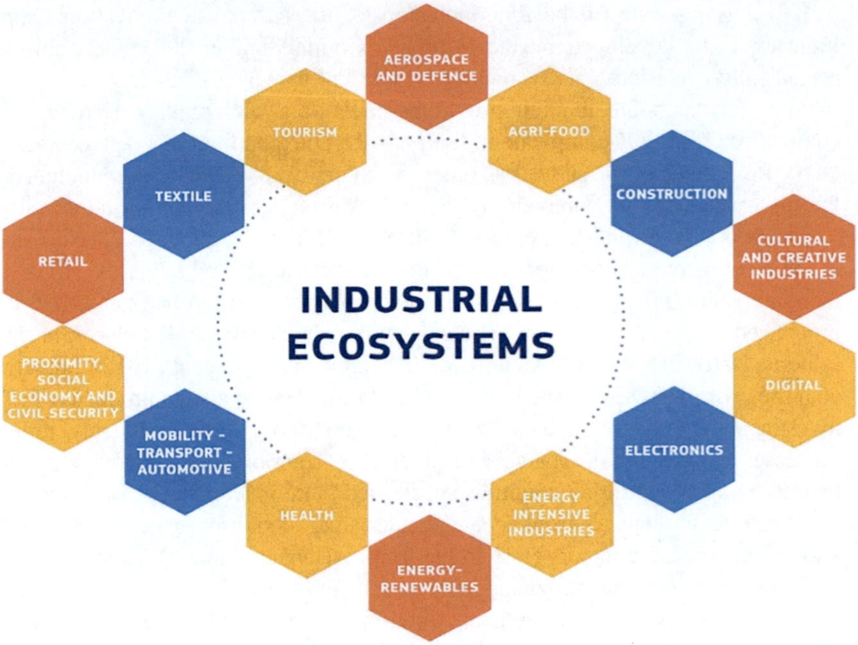

Fig. 5.2 The 14 industrial ecosystems of the EU Single Market. Source: https://commission.europa.eu/strategy-and-policy/priorities-2019-2024/europe-fit-digital-age/european-industrial-strategy_en#resilience-of-the-single-market

14 industrial ecosystems, based on their economic and technological relevance and expected contribution to the decarbonisation, digitalisation and resilience of the EU economy (Fig. 5.2). The 14 industrial ecosystems represent approximately 70% of the EU economy and 80% of the business economy (as a share of value added): (1) Aerospace and defence; (2) Agrifood; (3) Construction; (4) Cultural and Creative Industries; (5) Digital; (6) Electronics; (7) Energy-intensive industries; (8) Energy-Renewables; (9) Health; (10) Mobility-Transport-Automotive; (11) Proximity, Social economy and Civil security; (12) Retail; (13) Textiles; and (14) Tourism.

The 14 industrial ecosystems have been further categorised in three main groups—(i) technology-generating industrial ecosystems, (ii) technology uptake-oriented industries and (iii) service ecosystems—to better differentiate between technology-oriented and service-oriented ecosystems (Table 5.2).

The 2023 and 2024 editions of the Annual Single Market Report (European Commission, 2023b; European Commission, 2024) introduced a detailed analysis for each individual ecosystem based on the data provided by the European Monitor of Industrial Ecosystems (EMI) that serves as a key tool to monitor and assess trends in the implementation of the green and digital transition across the industrial ecosystems (European Commission, 2023a).

Table 5.2 Ecosystem definitions and levels of analysis

Industrial ecosystem	Definition
Technology-generating industrial ecosystems	
Aerospace and defence	The Aerospace and defence ecosystem covers manufacturing companies in aeronautics, space and defence; space operators and data and service providers; research institutes
Digital	The Digital ecosystem covers ICT manufacturing, services (excluding telecommunications) and telecommunications. ICT services account for the 95% of the total ICT value added
Electronics	The Electronics ecosystem covers design and manufacturing of electronic components and includes raw materials (semiconductor wafers) and manufacturing tools. The value chain stretches from design to semiconductor manufacturing to 'assembly-test-packaging' facilities, before reaching end-user companies, which integrate the chips into their product solution. Materials, equipment and related services and tools, including specific design tools and so-called functional blocks, enable design and manufacturing
Healthcare	Manufacturing of pharmaceuticals and their key inputs, medical devices and equipment and personal protective equipment; healthcare services (medical and residential care); health tech and related services. Companies are often part of global and complex supply chains
Mobility, Transport, and Automotive	The Mobility, Transport and Automotive ecosystem covers automotive, rail and waterborne. It is characterised by long and complex supply chain. The ecosystem is dominated by a few players that became global players
Energy/renewable energy	Renewables include wind energy, solar energy (photovoltaics, thermal and concentrated solar power), hydropower, bioenergy (including sustainable biofuels), geothermal energy, ocean energy and heat pumps. Furthermore, sustainable energy storage solutions, smart infrastructure technologies and energy conversion technologies, including electrolysers, are an important part of a clean energy ecosystem
Technology uptake-oriented industries	
Construction	The Construction ecosystem covers contractors for building and infrastructure projects, some construction product manufacturers, engineering and architectural services as well as a range of other economic activities (e.g. rental and leasing of machinery and equipment, employment agencies)
Agrifood	The Agrifood ecosystem covers all operators in the food supply chain (farmers, food industry, food retail and wholesale and food service) and their suppliers of inputs and services (seeds, pesticides, fertiliser, machinery, packaging, repair, transport, finance, advice and logistics)
Energy-intensive industries	The Energy-intensive industries (EIIs) ecosystem covers chemicals, steel, paper, plastics, mining, extraction and quarrying, refineries, cement, wood, rubber, nonferrous metals, glass and ceramics. They supply intermediate products to each other and to many downstream sectors of the economy and are closely integrated with energy providers as well as with the waste and recycling industries due to their need for secondary raw materials

(continued)

Table 5.2 (continued)

Industrial ecosystem	Definition
Textiles	The Textiles ecosystem includes transformation of natural (e.g. cotton, flax, wool), man-made and artificial (synthetic polyester and viscose) fibres into yarns and fabrics, production of yarns, home textiles, industrial filters, technical textiles, carpets and clothing. The ecosystem also includes production of footwear and leather. The ecosystem is particularly competitive in high-end clothing and technical textile for automotive applications, medical textile, agro textile and protective clothing. Most companies operate in complex value chains, making them dependent on external supplies, which can easily be disrupted
Service ecosystems	
Creative and Cultural Industries (CCIs)	The CCIs are a varied group. The biggest industries are audiovisual (TV, videogames, VOD, cinema, VR/AR), music, books and press publishing, advertising, cultural heritage (museums, historical sites), performance (theatre, dance) and visual arts
Proximity and Social Economy	The 'social economy' encompasses a variety of businesses, organisations and legal forms, including non-profit associations, cooperatives, mutual societies, foundations and social enterprises. They share the objective of systematically putting people first and producing a positive impact on local communities. The 'proximity economy' includes services and businesses fostering local and short value chains for mainly local production and consumption. Proximity businesses include local SMEs operating personal and contact services, small shops, bars and restaurants, repair, cleaning, maintenance services, etc.
Retail	Retail (large companies, SMEs, online and offline), relevant wholesale, online platforms. E-commerce represents 10–15% of total retail sales (much less for grocery retail). Market concentration differs across EU. The largest are mainly grocery chains, cosmetics, textiles and furniture sellers. Most important e-commerce players come from outside the EU. The performance of the ecosystem is key for household budgets and suppliers.
Tourism	In the EU, service providers at destination level (hospitality, attractions) are, in their majority, small local owners. Part of them are franchisees of a few multinational companies providing branding, marketing, management and selling services. The sector of cross-border passenger transporters is consolidating around a large operator (airlines and cruises in particular) but to a lesser extent than in the USA or China. They distribute their services directly or through travel agencies

Source: European Commission (2023a), pp. 40–41

In addition to its value for the sectoral analysis of EU's competitiveness, the 'industrial ecosystems' concept is relevant to our analysis for its capacity to introduce *a systemic innovation perspective to the Single Market*. We conceptualise thus the Single Market as an *innovation system* with the specific structural and functional format described in the innovation systems theory, consisting of components, relationships between components and functions, in the sense of competencies of the system components that determine the system's performance (Carlsson & Stankiewicz, 1991; Carlsson et al., 2002; Edquist, 2005; Bergek et al., 2008). The industrial ecosystems, as components of the Single Market innovation system, are themselves *a set of interconnected sectoral innovation systems and technological innovation systems that co-evolve within the boundaries of the Single Market national and regional innovation systems*. This vision is fully justified by analytical conceptualisations of these types of systems provided in the literature (Fig. 5.3).

The technological innovation systems mentioned above are being developed around the green and digital technologies that operate within and across the industrial ecosystems (Table 5.3). The share of companies adopting digital and green technologies (share in total companies) in each industrial ecosystem provides a relevant measure of the respective technologies' uptake in the respective industrial ecosystems (Table 5.4).

Strict boundaries of these types of innovation systems within the Single Market are difficult to delineate, considering the multiple interactions among the industrial ecosystems.[2] A particular technology may originate from research and innovation carried out in research institutes, universities or companies of one country or region (or internationally) and diffuse across other countries and regions, being relevant to various industrial sectors in a direct or indirect way, influencing price, market structures or new market formation for that technology or related ones (see, e.g. the example of solar cells in Hekkert et al., 2007). New technologies emerge in industrial sectors of national and regional economies where existing technologies, organisations, institutional structures, technological specialisations and policies determine the trajectory of the novel technology and its success or failure (Dosi, 1982; Pavitt, 1984; Castelacci, 2009; Wirth & Markard, 2011). National and regional innovation systems can significantly influence technology generation and diffusion in various industrial sectors through their actors and institutions' knowledge and technological innovation capabilities, density of networks and collaborative links among the actors, research and innovation capacity and many other factors that together constitute the absorptive capacity of a country or region and their capacity to embrace technological change.

Considering the Single Market industrial ecosystems as interconnected sectoral and technological innovation systems, the activities that occur within and among them constitute *functions of an innovation system* (Hekkert et al., 2007; Bergek et al., 2008) and can be analysed through specific indicators that characterise innovative economic and socio-technical transformations (Figs. 5.4 and 5.5).

[2] As Archibugi and Lundvall's (2002) note: '...it is useful to think in terms of "technological systems" as a special version of innovation systems. A technological system is a combination of interrelated sectors and firms, a set of institutions and regulations characterizing the rules of behaviour, and the knowledge infrastructure connected to it' (Archibugi & Lundvall, 2002, p. X).

Industrial ecosystems	"Industrial ecosystems are here defined as multi-tiered production systems involving heterogeneous agents operating in *sectoral value chains* and contributing to the *capability domains* of the ecosystem (and its participants) with closely complementary but dissimilar sets of resources and capabilities. The geographical boundaries of the industrial ecosystem are shaped by the evolving interdependencies linking organisations within the ecosystem and by the new linkages consolidating beyond that. Thus, the industrial ecosystem is a structured production space centred mainly on its productive organisations, as well as other institutions, intermediaries, and demand-side actors, purposefully involved in co-value creation processes along various types of diversification and innovative industrial renewal trajectories" (Andreoni 2018, p.1).
Sectoral innovation systems	"A sectoral system is a set of products and the set of agents carrying out market and non-market interactions for the creation, production, and sale of those products. A sectoral system has a specific knowledge base, technologies, inputs, and demand. Agents are individuals and organizations at various levels of aggregation. They interact through processes of communication, exchange, co-operation, competition and command, and these interactions are shaped by institutions. A sectoral system undergoes change and transformation through the co-evolution of its various elements ". (Malerba 2002, p. 1).
Technological systems	"A technological system is defined as a network of agents interacting in a specific economic/industrial area under a particular institutional infrastructure or set of infrastructures and involved in the generation, diffusion, and utilization of technology. Technological systems are defined in terms of knowledge/competence flows rather than flows of ordinary goods and services. In the presence of an entrepreneur and sufficient critical mass, such networks can be transformed into development blocks, i. e. synergistic clusters of firms and technologies which give rise to new business opportunities." (Carlsson and Stankiewicz 1991, p. 111)
Technological innovation systems	"Technological innovation systems (TIS) [are] socio-technical systems focused on the development, diffusion, and use of a particular technology (in terms of knowledge, product, or both). TISs do not only contain components exclusively dedicated to the technology in focus, but all components that influence the innovation process for that technology. A TIS may be a sub-system of a sectoral system (when the focus is one of the sector's products or a knowledge field that is exclusive to the sector) or may cut across several sectors (when the focus is a more "generic" knowledge field that several sectors make use of, e.g., microwave technology). TISs may have a geographical dimension but are often international in nature." (Bergek et al. 2008, pp. 408-409)
Regional innovation systems	"The regional innovation system can be thought of as the institutional infrastructure supporting innovation within the production structure of a region" (Asheim and Coenen 2005, p. 1177)

Fig. 5.3 Industrial ecosystems and innovation systems. Source: own elaboration

	"The best configuration of a Regional Innovation System can be evaluated from a dual perspective: (a) From a regionalisation approach, relating the region to its competence (jurisdiction) capacity, valuing its degree of autonomy to develop policies and manage the different elements that make up the regional system, as well as financing capacity for strategic investments in infrastructures necessary for the development of innovation processes. (b) From a regionalism approach, related to the region's cultural base which gives it a certain level of systemic potential. … Finally, regional innovation systems were conceptualised in terms of a collective order based on micro-constitutional regulation conditioned by trust, reliability, exchange, and cooperative interaction." (Cooke 1997, pp. 489-490)
National innovation system	". . an open, evolving and complex system that encompasses relationships within and between organizations, institutions and socio-economic structures which determine the rate and direction of innovation and competence-building emanating from processes of science-based and experience-based learning. (Lundvall et al., 2009, p. 7)

Fig. 5.3 (continued)

Table 5.3 Overview of technologies operating across the industrial ecosystems

DIGITAL TRANSFORMATION	
Basic digital	Online platform
	Software
Advanced digital	Advanced manufacturing and robotics Advanced manufacturing (ICA and mechanical engineering) Robotics
	Artificial intelligence
	Augmented and virtual reality
	Big data and cloud computing
	Blockchain
	Digital security and networks/cybersecurity
	Internet of Things
	Micro- and nanoelectronics and photonics
GREEN TRANSFORMATION	
Green technologies	Advanced materials
	Biotechnology
	Energy-saving technologies
	Renewable energy technologies Solar power Wind power Other (geothermal, hydropower, biomass)
	Clean production technologies
	Recycling and waste management technologies
Circular business models	Remanufacturing Renting, leasing and related service models Repair and maintenance services Resell, reuse Circular design (products that can be disassembled and recycled) Design for durability (products that can last longer)

Source: European Commission (2023a), pp. 41–42

Table 5.4 Companies adopting digital and green technologies (share in total companies). Data collected during the period March to June 2023 (following Annual Single Market Report 2021 ecosystem definitions). Dataset: EMI survey 2023, Last updated: May 2023, Geographical scope: EU27

Twin transition	Technologies	Aerospace and defence	Agrifood	Tourism	Cultural and creative industries	Construction	Electronics	Energy-intensive industries	Health	Mobility	Proximity, social economy	Retail	Textiles
Digital	Artificial intelligence	0.14	0.11	0.08	0.10	0.10	0.06	0.13	0.14	0.10	0.03	0.06	0.08
Digital	Augmented and virtual reality	0.13	0.07	0.04	0.08	0.11	0.10	0.07	0.07	0.10	0.01	0.03	0.08
Digital	Big data	0.24	0.17	0.14	0.12	0.14	0.11	0.14	0.15	0.11	0.03	0.10	0.13
Digital	Blockchain	0.04	0.05	0.02	0.02	0.04	0.05	0.04	0.05	0.04	0.02	0.05	0.04
Digital	Cloud technologies	0.30	0.27	0.25	0.20	0.27	0.16	0.29	0.31	0.20	0.14	0.19	0.32
Digital	Digital twin	0.10	0.09	0.06	0.07	0.08	0.06	0.07	0.03	0.10	0.00	0.05	0.05
Digital	Internet of Things	0.12	0.10	0.10	0.08	0.13	0.07	0.12	0.20	0.07	0.07	0.10	0.14
Digital	Online platform	0.22	0.30	0.29		0.24	0.17	0.27		0.22			
Digital	Robotics	0.16	0.11	0.02	0.04	0.05	0.11	0.09	0.17	0.08	0.01	0.01	0.09
Green	Additive manufacturing	0.09	0.13	NA	0.10	0.13	0.09	0.12		0.11		0.01	0.07
Green	Advanced sustainable materials (bio-based, organic)	0.09	0.28	0.21	0.09	0.10	0.06	0.17	0.23	0.20	0.03	0.03	0.23
Green	Biotechnology		0.20	NA		0.07	0.04	0.10			0.04	0.01	0.08
Green	Carbon capture technologies	0.06	0.12	0.11	0.04	0.08	0.06	0.10	0.17	0.12	0.03	0.01	0.06

Green	Clean production technologies	0.12	0.29	NA	0.11	0.15	0.08	0.18	0.25	0.13	0.03	0.05	0.24
Green	Energy-saving technologies	0.26	0.34	0.29	0.19	0.23	0.14	0.19	0.15	0.20	0.10	0.14	0.28
Green	Food waste reduction measures		0.27	0.26									
Green	Recycled materials	0.20	0.32	0.31	0.20	0.22	0.12	0.20	0.24	0.19	0.08	0.12	0.32
Green	Recycling technologies	0.16	0.32	0.21	0.17	0.20	0.11	0.20	0.24	0.19	0.09	0.11	0.24
Green	Renewable energies	0.12	0.28	0.24	0.14	0.20	0.13	0.17	0.24	0.16	0.18	0.10	0.18
Green	Waste reduction technologies		0.23	0.19					0.20				0.16
Green	Water reduction technologies		0.27	0.24					0.20				

Source: European Commission (2023a). EMI Data Package Aerospace and Defence.xlsx (live.com)

Fig. 5.4 The seven functions of an innovation system. Source: own elaboration based on Hekkert et al. (2007)

System function	Mapping indicators
Entrepreneurial activities: translation of new knowledge, networks, and markets into new business opportunities by entrepreneurs who perform market-oriented experiments that establish change, both to the emerging technology and to the institutions that surround it. Entrepreneurial experiments can help clarify various uncertainties, learn about technologies and markets, reactions of consumers, government, competitors, and suppliers. The presence of active entrepreneurs is a good indication of a good performance of the innovation system.	New entrants, diversification activities of incumbent actors, experiments with the new technology, projects proving the usefulness of the emerging technology in a practical and/or commercial environment (experiments, demonstrations)
Knowledge development: learning activities on emerging technologies, markets, networks, users etc. That can include both learning-by-searching (R&D activities in basic science, inventions) and learning-by-doing (lab experiments, adoption trials). Mostly in universities and research institutions.	R&D projects, patents, and investments in R&D, increase in technological performance by means of 'learning curves'.
Knowledge diffusion/exchange through networks: activities that facilitate knowledge exchange between all the network components.	Partnerships between actors, number of workshops and conferences devoted to a specific technology topic, network size and intensity over time, patents, learning-by-using (users of technological innovations, e. g. through user-producer interactions)
Guidance of the search: can be performed by a variety of system components such as industry, government, market.	Specific policy or investment targets by governments or industries regarding the use of specific technologies; activities that can positively affect the visibility and clarity of specific needs among users; articles in professional journals that raise expectations about new technological developments; regulations and policies; changing prices, assessments of market opportunities, crises, promises and expectations expressed by various actors in the community.
Market formation: Activities that contribute to the creation of demand (financial support for the use of emerging technologies, mapping the number of niche markets, specific tax regimes for new technologies and for the use of competing technologies, new environmental standards that improve the chances for	Number of niche markets introduced, specific tax regimes for new technologies, new environmental standards that improve the chances for new environmental technologies

Fig. 5.5 Innovation system functions and mapping indicators. Source: selected from Hekkert et al. (2007)

new environmental technologies, sustainable energy technologies.	
Resource mobilisation: financial, human, and material resources, infrastructures	Allocation of investments and subsidies, long-term R&D programmes set up by industry or government to develop specific technological knowledge, human capital to support an emerging technology, testing of new technologies in niche experiments, deployment of educational systems, large R&D facilities or infrastructures, natural resources, such as biomass, oil, natural gas.
Creation of Legitimacy/Counteracting resistance to change: support from advocacy coalitions and interest groups to counteract resistance from actors with interests in the incumbent system, e. g. by urging authorities to reorganize the institutional configuration of the system, political lobbies, advice on behalf of interest groups.	Rise and growth of interest groups and their lobby actions.

Fig. 5.5 (continued)

References

Adner, R. (2017). Ecosystem as structure: An actionable construct for strategy. *Journal of Management, 43*(1), 39–58. https://doi.org/10.1177/0149206316678451

Andreoni, A. (2018). The architecture and dynamics of industrial ecosystems: Diversification and innovative industrial renewal in Emilia Romagna. *Cambridge Journal of Economics, 42*(6), 1613–1642. https://doi.org/10.1093/cje/bey037

Archibugi, D., & Lundvall, B.-A. (Eds.). (2002). *The globalizing learning economy*. Oxford University Press. (Oxford, 2002; online edn, Oxford Academic, 1 Nov. 2003). https://doi.org/10.1093/0199258171.001.0001

Asheim, B. T., & Coenen, L. (2005). Knowledge bases and regional innovation systems: Comparing Nordic clusters. *Research Policy, 34*(8), 1173–1190. https://doi.org/10.1016/j.respol.2005.03.013

Autio, E., Nambisan, S., Thomas, L. D. W., & Wright, M. (2018). Digital affordances, spatial affordances, and the genesis of entrepreneurial ecosystems. *Strategic Entrepreneurship Journal, 12*(1), 72–95. https://doi.org/10.1002/sej.1266

Bergek, A., Jacobsson, S., Carlsson, B., Lindmark, S., & Rickne, A. (2008). Analysing the functional dynamics of technological innovation systems: A scheme of analysis. *Research Policy, 37*(3), 407–429. https://doi.org/10.1016/j.respol.2007.12.003

Carlsson, B., & Stankiewicz, R. (1991). On the nature, function and composition of technological systems. *Journal of Evolutionary Economics, 1*(2), 93–118. https://doi.org/10.1007/BF01224915

Carlsson, B., Jacobsson, S., Holmén, M., & Rickne, A. (2002). Innovation systems: Analytical and methodological issues. *Research Policy, 31*, 233–245. https://doi.org/10.1016/S0048-7333(01)00138-X

Castelacci, F. (2009). The interactions between national systems and sectoral patterns of innovation: AA cross-country analysis of Pavitt's taxonomy. *Journal of Evolutionary Economics, 19*(3), 321–347. https://doi.org/10.1007/s00191-008-0113-9

Cooke, P., Uranga, G. M., & Etxebarria, G. (1997). Regional systems of innovation: Institutional and Organisational dimensions. *Research Policy, 26*, 475–491. https://doi.org/10.1016/S0048-7333(97)00025-5

Dosi, G. (1982). Technological paradigms and technological trajectories: A suggested interpretation of the determinants and directions of technical change. *Research Policy, 11*(3), 147–162. https://doi.org/10.1016/0048-7333(82)90016-6

Edquist, C. (2005). Systems of Innovation: Perspectives and challenges. In J. Fagerberg, D. Mowery, & R. R. Nelson (Eds.), *Oxford handbook of innovation* (pp. 181–208). Oxford University Press. ISBN 978-0-19-926455-1.

European Commission. (2020). COM(2020) 102 final. *A new industrial strategy for Europe*. https://eur-lex.europa.eu/legal-content/EN/TXT/?uri=CELEX:52020DC0102

European Commission. (2021). COM(2021) 350 final. *Annual single market report 2021. Updating the 2020 new industrial strategy: Building a stronger single market for Europe's recovery*. https://commission.europa.eu/document/download/9ab0244c-6ca3-4b11-bef9-422c7eb34f39_en?filename=communication-industrial-strategy-update-2020_en.pdf

European Commission. (2023). COM(2023) 168 final. *Long-term competitiveness of the EU: looking beyond 2030*. https://commission.europa.eu/system/files/2023-03/Communication_Long-term-competitiveness.pdf

European Commission. (2023a). *Monitoring European industrial ecosystems. Conceptual, monitoring and indicator framework*. https://monitor-industrial-ecosystems.ec.europa.eu/sites/default/files/2023-12/EMI%20Methodological%20Report.pdf.

European Commission. (2023b). SWD(2023) 26 final. *2023 Annual single market report: Single market at 30*. https://single-market-economy.ec.europa.eu/system/files/2023-01/ASMR 2023.pdf

European Commission. (2024). COM(2024) 77 final. *The 2024 annual single market and competitiveness report*. https://eur-lex.europa.eu/legal-content/EN/TXT/?uri=CELEX%3A52024DC0077

Hekkert, M. P., Suurs, R. A. A., Negro, S. O., Kuhlmann, S., & Smits, R. E. H. M. (2007). Functions of innovation systems: A new approach for analysing technological change. *Technological Forecasting and Social Change, 74*(4), 413–432. https://doi.org/10.1016/j.techfore.2006.03.002

Janger, J., Schubert, T., Andries, P., Rammer, C., & Hoskens, M. (2017). The EU 2020 innovation indicator: A step forward in measuring innovation outputs and outcomes? *Research Policy, 46*(1), 30–42. https://doi.org/10.1016/j.respol.2016.10.001

Korhonen, J. (2001). Four ecosystem principles for an industrial ecosystem. *Journal of Cleaner Production, 9*(3), 253–259. https://doi.org/10.1016/S0959-6526(00)00058-5

Lowe, E. A., & Evans, L. K. (1995). Industrial ecology and industrial ecosystems. *Journal of Cleaner Production, 3*(1), 47–53. https://doi.org/10.1016/0959-6526(95)00045-G

Lundvall, B.-Å., Vang, J., Joseph, K., & Chaminade, C. (2009). Innovation system research and developing countries. In B.-Å. Lundvall, K. J. Joseph, C. Chaminade, & J. Vang (Eds.), *Handbook of innovation systems and developing countries: Building domestic capabilities in a global setting*. Edward Elgar.

Malerba, F. (2002). Sectoral systems of innovation and production. *Research Policy, 31*(2), 247–264. https://doi.org/10.1016/S0048-7333(01)00139-1

Mathieu, A., & van Pottelsberghe de la Potterie, B. (2010). A note on the drivers of R&D intensity. *Research in World Economy, 1*, 56–65. https://doi.org/10.5430/rwe.v1n1p56

Pavitt, K. (1984). Sectoral patterns of technical change: Towards a taxonomy and a theory. *Research Policy, 13*(6), 343–373. https://doi.org/10.1016/0048-7333(84)90018-0

Reinstaller, A., & Unterlass, F. (2012). Comparing business R&D across countries over time: A decomposition exercise using data for the EU 27. *Applied Economics Letters, 19*(12), 1143–1148. https://doi.org/10.1080/13504851.2011.615724

Renda, A. (2024, April 2024). *What North Star for future EU industrial policy? CEPS In-Depth Analysis.* https://cdn.ceps.eu/wp-content/uploads/2024/04/CEPS-InDepthAnalysis-2024-07_EU-North-Star-for-EU-Industrial-Policy-3.pdf

Wirth, S., & Markard, J. (2011). Context matters: How existing sectors and competing technologies affect the prospects of the Swiss bio-SNG innovation system. *Technological Forecasting and Social Change, 78*(4), 635–649. https://doi.org/10.1016/j.techfore.2011.01.001

Chapter 6
European Green Deal Effects on the Single Market from an 'Innovation System' Perspective

Abstract In this chapter, the analytical framework of innovation system functions is applied to assess the impact of the European Green Deal on the Single Market industrial ecosystems. Several indicators and activities selected from multiple sources are used to explore each function across the 14 industrial ecosystems. The findings reveal an ample impact of the European Green Deal on the Single Market's industrial ecosystems. However, the uneven concentration of R&I projects and EU R&D funding for the green and digital transitions across the ecosystems may have the unintended effect of creating new imbalances at the level of the Single Market as a whole, and affect the economic performance and capacity of the ecosystems with low levels of such investments to implement green and digital technologies in the longer run. This deficit is compensated to a limited some extent by the indirect benefits derived from the economic links with the other ecosystems and the investment provided through other instruments, such as the Recovery and Resilience Plans.

In this chapter, the analytical framework of the innovation system functions described in Chap. 5 is applied to examine effects of the European Green Deal on the Single Market and its industrial ecosystems. Several types of quantitative and qualitative data have been used as mapping indicators for each function of the innovation system, as suggested by Hekkert et al. (2007), and have been examined across the industrial ecosystems (Table 6.1):

- *Projects focused on the green and digital transitions funded by the EU research and innovation (R&I) programmes*

M. Ranga, *Single Market 2.0*, Contributions to Economics,
https://doi.org/10.1007/978-3-031-83220-8_6

- Projects selected under Horizon 2020 European Green Deal call (2014–2020).
- Projects selected under Horizon Europe (2021–2027) called European Partnerships. They were associated with the Green Missions[1] and were financed under the Horizon Europe's first Strategic Plan 2021–2024.

Both groups of projects and related information have been identified by own search on the EU Funding & Tenders Portal,[2] dedicated European Commission websites and individual project websites.

- *Data provided by European Monitor of Industrial Ecosystems*,[3] which is used by the European Commission as a key tool for monitoring and assessing trends regarding the implementation of the green and digital transition across industrial ecosystems. Several types of data for the 14 industrial ecosystems are provided at EMI Data Package Agri-Food.xlsx (live.com).
- *Data provided by evaluation reports* of the Horizon 2020 European Green Deal call and the overall Horizon 2020 ex-post evaluation, as well as the biennial evaluation of Horizon Europe European Partnerships, conducted by the European Commission.
- *Data on various programmes and initiatives related to the two types of R&I projects mentioned above*, promoted by the European Commission and the private sector, selected from dedicated websites.

Table 6.1 Mapping indicators for the seven functions of the Single Market as an innovation system

System function	Data
Knowledge development	• R&I projects focused on the green and digital transition financed through Horizon 2020 and Horizon Europe, per industrial ecosystem (dedicated EC websites) • EU R&D funding for projects focused on the green and digital transition, per industrial ecosystem (EMI) • Professionals with digital and green transition skills employed in industrial ecosystems (share in total professionals) (EMI)

(continued)

[1] The Green Missions represent four out the five missions defined by Horizon Europe that are directly related to the European Green Deal: (i) Adaptation to Climate Change: support at least 150 European regions and communities to become climate resilient by 2030; (ii) Restore Our Ocean and Waters by 2030; (iii) 100 Climate-Neutral and Smart Cities by 2030; and (iv) A Soil Deal for Europe: 100 living labs and lighthouses to lead the transition towards healthy soils by 2030 (Source: https://research-and-innovation.ec.europa.eu/funding/funding-opportunities/funding-programmes-and-open-calls/horizon-europe/eu-missions-horizon-europe_en).

[2] https://ec.europa.eu/info/funding-tenders/opportunities/portal/screen/opportunities/projects-results?isExactMatch=true&order=DESC&pageNumber=1&pageSize=10&sortBy=title

[3] https://monitor-industrial-ecosystems.ec.europa.eu/

Table 6.1 (continued)

System function	Data
Knowledge diffusion/exchange through networks	• Structure and collaborative activities of the consortia and networks developed by the R&I projects financed under the European Green Deal call of Horizon 2020 and the European Partnerships of Horizon Europe (EC evaluation reports)
Market formation	• Activities focused on experimentation, demonstration, formation of niche markets and development of new/disruptive technologies that ensure Europe's leadership and technological sovereignty performed within the R&I projects financed under the European Green Deal call of Horizon 2020 and the European Partnerships of Horizon Europe (EC evaluation reports)
Entrepreneurial activity	• Activities performed within the R&I projects financed under the European Green Deal call of Horizon 2020 and the European Partnerships of Horizon Europe to support SMEs and entrepreneurs (EC evaluation reports)
Resource mobilisation	• Funding mobilised from the EC, national budgets and the private sector and their multi-annual allocation by the R&I projects financed under the European Green Deal call of Horizon 2020 and the European Partnerships of Horizon Europe (EC evaluation reports)
Guidance of the search	• Activities of the European Commission (conceptual design, implementation rules, funding allocations) that ensure the governance of the European Green Deal call of Horizon 2020 and the European Partnerships of Horizon Europe (dedicated EC websites) • Activities performed within selected European Partnerships of Horizon Europe that contribute to setting industry trends, policymaking by influencing changes in regulations and policies and encouraging government support for specific industries or technologies, etc. • Long-term R&I programmes and initiatives developed by leading industry players for the development and use of specific technologies
Creation of legitimacy/counteracting resistance to change	• Activities performed within the R&I projects financed under the Horizon 2020 European Green Deal call to build support from advocacy coalitions and interest groups for counteracting resistance from actors with interests in the incumbent system, e.g. citizen events, political lobbies, etc.

Source: own elaboration

6.1 Function: Knowledge Development

The mapping indicators used to analyse this function are briefly described below.

A. Projects focused on the green and digital transition selected under the Horizon 2020 European Green call and Horizon Europe—European Partnerships

   – The Horizon 2020 European Green Deal call

This call, the last and largest of Horizon 2020, was open from September 2020 to January 2021 and followed closely the European Green Deal both in structure and in approach. The structure consisted of 20 topics spread across 10 thematic areas, of which 8 thematic areas reflect the structure of the European Green Deal and 2 are horizontal thematic areas (Fig. 6.1). The approach of the call was two-sided: on the one hand, a strong focus on 'impact', by prioritising technology development and demonstration, pilot applications and demonstration projects, scalable innovative products and experiments, and, on the other, a focus on 'social' aspects, e.g. governance, cultural and behavioural aspects and social innovation, supporting civil society engagement. These two elements—structure and approach—that are

Areas	Topics
Thematic	
1. Increasing climate ambition: cross sectoral challenges	1.1. Preventing and fighting extreme wildfires with the integration and demonstration of innovative means 1.2. Towards climate-neutral and socially innovative cities 1.3. Climate-resilient innovation packages for EU regions
2. Clean, affordable and secure energy	2.1. Innovative land-based and offshore renewable energy technologies and their integration into the energy system 2.2. Develop and demonstrate a 100 MW electrolyser upscaling the link between renewables and industrial applications 2.3. Accelerating the green transition and energy access partnership with Africa
3. Industry for a clean and circular economy	3.1. Closing the industrial carbon cycle to combat climate change 3.2. Demonstration of systemic solutions for the territorial deployment of the circular economy
4. Energy and resource efficient buildings	4.1. Building and renovating in an energy and resource efficient way
5. Sustainable and smart mobility	5.1. Green airports and ports as multimodal hubs for sustainable and smart mobility
6. Farm to fork	6.1. Testing and demonstrating systemic innovations for sustainable food from farm to fork
7. Biodiversity and ecosystems	7.1. Restoring biodiversity and ecosystem services
8. Zero-pollution, toxic-free environments	8.1. Innovative, systemic zero-pollution solutions to protect health, environment and natural resources from persistent and mobile chemicals 8.2. Fostering regulatory science to address chemical and pharmaceutical mixtures: from science to evidence-based policies
Horizontal	
9. Strengthening knowledge	9.1. European Research Infrastructures' capacities and services to address European Green Deal challenges 9.2. Developing end-user products and services for all stakeholders and citizens supporting climate adaptation and mitigation 9.3. A transparent and accessible ocean: towards a digital twin of the ocean
10. Empowering citizens	10.1. European capacities for citizen deliberation and participation for the Green Deal 10.2. Behavioural, social and cultural change for the Green Deal 10.3. Enabling citizens to act on climate change and environmental protection through education, citizen science, observation initiatives, and civic involvement

Fig. 6.1 Structure of Horizon 2020 Green Deal call. Source: European Commission (2020), p. 2

quite different from other Horizon 2020 calls, reflected the ambition of this call to demonstrate that research and innovation can provide concrete solutions to the European Green Deal challenges within a relatively short time frame (European Commission, 2021). The call selected 73 projects with a short- to medium-term time frame from autumn 2021 to various end points during 2024–2027 that were organized into 5 working groups (Fig. 6.2): ‘Clean Energy’ (16 projects), ‘Climate Change and Biodiversity’ (17 projects), ‘Food and Health’ (15 projects: 9 Food and 6 Health), ‘Urban Environment and Mobility’ (9 projects), and ‘Knowledge and Citizens’ (16 projects).[4]

– The European Partnerships of Horizon Europe (2021–2027)

The European (Green) Partnerships have been introduced as a new wave of projects in Horizon Europe, closely aligned with the European Green Deal objectives of accelerating the green and digital transitions while strengthening the resilience and competitiveness of European industry. This approach aimed to simplify the Horizon Europe architecture; provide more directionality, additionality, transparency, openness, coherence and synergies to the investments made under the European Green Deal and Digital Europe; engage a broader set of stakeholders across the EU and beyond; and establish closer links with EU and national policies (European Commission, 2022).

In the first Strategic Plan of Horizon Europe 2021–2024, 49 projects have been selected as European Partnerships (Fig. 6.3) associated with the Green Missions. Most of these projects (38) are part of the thematic clusters of Pillar II ‘Global Challenges and European Industrial Competitiveness’, as follows:

- Cluster 1: ‘Health’ (9 projects)
- Cluster 4: ‘Digital, industry and space’ (10 projects)
- Cluster 5: ‘Climate, energy and mobility’ (11 projects)
- Cluster 6: ‘Food, bioeconomy, natural resources, agriculture and environment’ (8 projects)

Clusters 5 and 6 contribute mainly to the green transition (Fig. 6.4), while Cluster 4 contributes mainly to the digital transition and industrial leadership (Fig. 6.5), but there are significant synergies and potential for cooperation between Clusters 4, 5 and 6, as well as with the other clusters.

The European Partnerships include three types of projects—co-programmed, co-funded and institutionalized—that differ in terms of their preparation, functioning and overall impact (Table 6.2). Our analysis will consider only the 38 projects associated with Pillar II, as the projects associated with Pillar III refer to the Knowledge and Innovation Communities (KICs) of the European Institute of Innovation and Technology (EIT).

---

[4]Details on these projects by Working Group are available at https://ec.europa.eu/research-and-innovation/en/strategy/strategy-2020-2024/environment-and-climate/european-green-deal/green-deal-projects-support/green-deal-projects-working-groups.

Fig. 6.2 Projects selected under the Horizon 2020 European Green Deal call by working group. Source: selected from https://ec.europa.eu/research-and-innovation/en/strategy/strategy-2020-2024/environment-and-climate/european-green-deal/green-deal-projects-support/green-deal-projects-working-groups

Fig. 6.3 Structure of Horizon Europe European Partnerships, First Strategic Plan (2021–2024). Source: European Commission (2022), p. 5

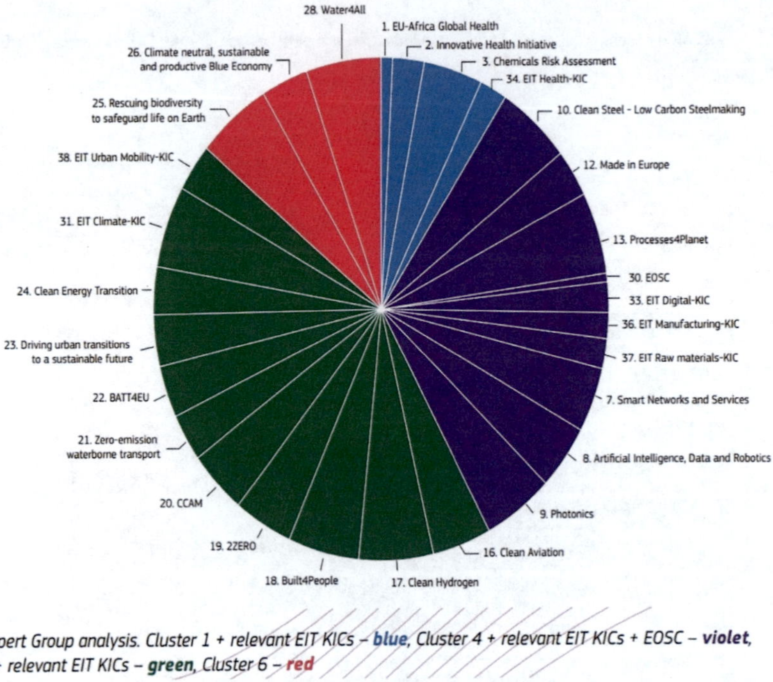

Fig. 6.4 Contribution of all active Horizon Europe European Partnerships to the green transition. Source: European Commission (2022a), p. 53

B. EU R&D funding for projects focused on the green and digital transition (million EURO)—the data is provided by European Monitor of Industrial Ecosystems (EMI) (European Commission, 2023), based on a selection from the CORDIS database[5] (last updated October 2023), and refers to two types of projects:

– *Projects under Horizon 2020 (2014–2020) in the 'Industrial Leadership' pillar*—this is one of the three pillars of Horizon 2020, with a total budget of EUR 17,015 million for investments along three axes[6]:

Leadership in enabling and industrial technologies (LEITs)—EUR 13,557 million: to support ICT, nanotechnologies, materials, biotechnology, manufacturing, space

Access to risk finance (EUR 2842 million): to leverage private finance and venture capital

Innovation in SMEs (EUR 616 million): to foster all forms of innovation in all types of SMEs

[5] See full methodological explanations in European Commission (2023), p. 28.

[6] https://ec.europa.eu/research/participants/docs/h2020-funding-guide/grants/applying-for-funding/find-a-call/h2020-structure-and-budget_en.htm

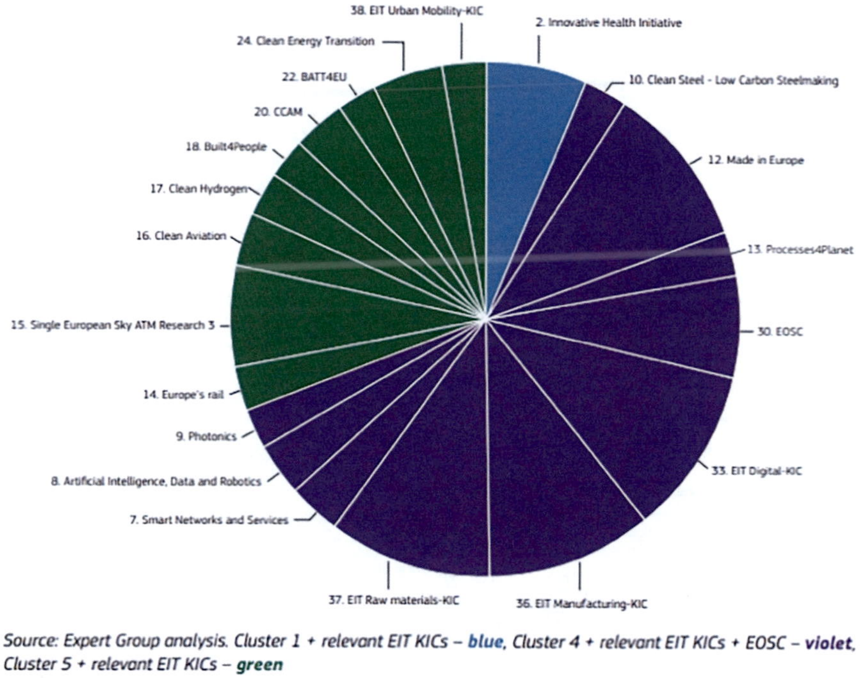

Fig. 6.5 Contribution of all active Horizon Europe European Partnerships to the digital transition. Source: European Commission (2022b), p. 59

– *Projects under Horizon Europe (2021–2027) in Cluster 4 'Digital, Industry and Space',* under Pillar II "Global Challenges and European Industrial Competitiveness"

Distribution of R&I Projects Focused on the Green and Digital Transitions, per Industrial Ecosystem

The distribution of R&I projects focused on the green and digital transitions financed by both Horizon 2020 European Green Deal call and Horizon Europe-European Partnerships across the 14 industrial ecosystems is presented in Fig. 6.6, with additional details on the project coverage for each ecosystem in Fig. 6.7.

Table 6.2 Types of European Partnerships in Horizon Europe and their key characteristics

Type	Legal form	Implementation
Co-programmed	Memoranda of Understanding between the EC and mostly private (sometimes public) partners	The EU contribution is implemented through a Framework Programme, and the partners' contributions are under their responsibilities. The EC approved 11 Co-Programmed Partnerships by June 2021, to run from 2021 to 2030 with a budget of over €8 billion from Horizon Europe. The partnerships also address the EU's digital transition, in line with Europe's Digital Decade
Co-funded	Grant Agreement between EU countries, research funders and other public authorities	The EU provides top-up funding for an integrated programme with distributed implementation by entities managing and/or funding national R&I programmes. There are 16 partnerships based on programme co-fund actions
Institutionalised	Between the EU, Member States and/or industry, based on Art 185/187 of TFEU and the EIT Regulation for 2021–2027	Integrated programmes with centralised implementation. Require legislative proposals from the EC and are implemented by dedicated structures created for that purpose, only where other parts of the Horizon Europe programme, including other types of partnership, would not achieve the desired objectives or expected impacts. Specific partnerships in this category are the *EIT Knowledge and Innovation Communities (KICs)* that are already established under Horizon 2020. Currently there are 11 institutionalised partnerships and 9 EIT KICs

Source: based on European Commission (2022), p.23 and European Partnerships in Horizon Europe (europa.eu)

Distribution of EU R&D Funding Across the Industrial Ecosystems

The European Monitor of Industrial Ecosystems (EMI) provides data on the EU R&D funding for projects focused on the green and digital transition per industrial ecosystem, as shown in Figs. 6.8 and 6.9.

Corroborating the insights from the distribution of R&I projects and EU R&D funding across the industrial ecosystems, one can observe a high concentration of both R&I projects and EU R&D funding in a few ecosystems: Energy-Renewables

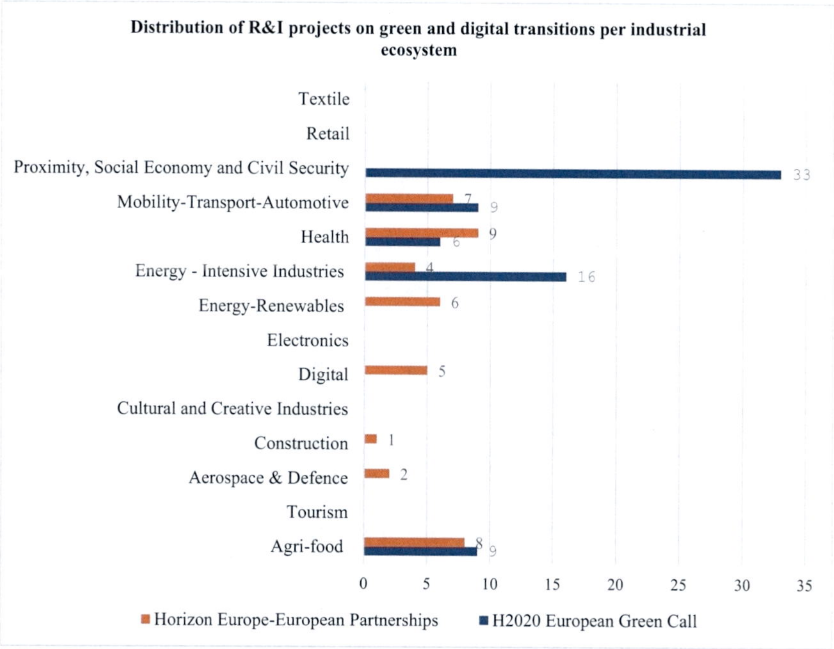

H2020 European Green Deal call -73 projects

Clean Energy (16 projects)

Food and health (15 projects: 9 Food, 6 Health)

Urban environment and mobility (9 projects)

Knowledge and citizens (16 projects)

Climate change and biodiversity (17 projects)

Horizon Europe European Partnerships (HE-EP) Pillar II- 38 projects:

Cluster 1: Health (9 projects)

Cluster 4: Digital, industry and space (10 projects)

Cluster 5: Climate, energy, and mobility (11 projects)

Cluster 6: Food, bioeconomy, natural resources, agriculture, and environment (8 projects)

Projects in Clusters 4 and 5 cover several industrial ecosystems, as shown in Figure 19.

Fig. 6.6 Distribution of R&I projects on the green and digital transitions financed by Horizon 2020 European Green Deal call and Horizon Europe European Partnerships, per industrial ecosystems. Source: own elaboration

and Energy-Intensive industries, Digital and Electronics, Agrifood and Health. These are followed by some low-to-moderate numbers of projects and R&D investments in the ecosystems Textile, Cultural and Creative Industries, Construction, and Tourism—while some ecosystems, such as Retail, have no such investments.

This uneven coverage of the 14 industrial ecosystems can be a result of several factors:

Agri-food	H2020 European Green Deal call - group 'Food and health' (9 projects on Food)
	Horizon Europe - European Partnerships (EP) Cluster 6'Food, bioeconomy, natural resources, agriculture and environment' (8 projects) • EP Accelerating farming systems transition: agroecology living labs and research infrastructure. • EP for Animal Health and Welfare (PAHW) • EP for Agriculture of Data • European Biodiversity Partnership (Biodiversa+) • EP for a climate neutral, sustainable and productive Blue Economy (SBEP) • EP for Safe and Sustainable Food Systems (FutureFoodS) • EP for a Circular bio-based Europe • EP Water security for the planet (Water4All)
Tourism	NA
Aerospace & Defence	Horizon Europe - European Partnerships (EP) Cluster 4 'Digital, industry and space' (1 project) • EP Globally Competitive Space Systems Cluster 5 'Climate, energy, and mobility' (1 project) • EP Clean Aviation
Construction	Horizon Europe - European Partnerships (EP) Cluster 5 'Climate, energy, and mobility' (1 project) • EP People-centric sustainable built environment (Built4People)
Digital /Electronics	Horizon Europe - European Partnerships (EP) Cluster 4 'Digital, industry and space' (5 projects) • EP High Performance Computing • EP Key Digital Technologies (KDT) • EP Smart Networks and Services • EP AI, Data and Robotics • EP Photonics
Energy - renewables	Horizon Europe - European Partnerships (EP) Cluster 5 'Climate, energy, and mobility' (6 projects) • EP Clean Hydrogen • EP People-centric sustainable built environment (Built4People) • EP Industrial Battery Value Chain (Batt4EU) • EP Clean Aviation • EP Driving urban transitions to a sustainable future (DUT) • EP Clean Energy Transition
Energy - Intensive Industries	H2020 European Green Deal call - group 'Clean Energy' (16 projects)
	Horizon Europe - European Partnerships (EP) Cluster 4 'Digital, industry and space' (4 projects) • EP Clean Steel – Low-Carbon Steelmaking • EP Metrology • EP Made in Europe (manufacturing) • EP Processes4Planet
Health	H2020 European Green Deal call - group 'Food and Health' (6 projects on Health)
	Horizon Europe - European Partnerships (EP) Cluster 1 - Health (9 projects)

Fig. 6.7 Overview of R&I projects on the green and digital transitions financed by Horizon 2020 European Green Deal call and Horizon Europe European Partnerships, per industrial ecosystem. Source: own elaboration

Mobility-Transport-Automotive	H2020 'Urban environment and mobility' (9 projects) Horizon Europe - European Partnerships (EP) Cluster 5 'Climate, energy, and mobility' (7 projects) • EP Driving urban transitions to a sustainable future (DUT) • EP Transforming Europe's rail system • EP Integrated Air Traffic Management • EP Clean Aviation • EP Connected, Cooperative and Automated Driving (CCAM) • EP Zero-emission waterborne transport • EP Towards zero-emission road transport (2ZERO)
Proximity, Soc. Economy and Civil Security	H2020 European Green Deal call - group 'Knowledge and citizens' (16 projects) and group 'Climate change and biodiversity' (17 projects)
Retail	NA
Textile	NA

Fig. 6.7 (continued)

Ecosystem	Green transition			Digital transition		
	H2020	Horizon Europe	Combined	H2020	Horizon Europe	Combined
Agri-food	486.59	100.73	587.32	242.08	35.87	277.95
Tourism	31.31	16.17	47.48	52.51	27.23	79.74
Aerospace & Defence	6.91	29.15	36.06	153.67	34.14	187.81
Construction	115.21	44.09	159.31	61.86	34.14	96.54
Cultural and Creative Industries	11.59	6	17.59	81.40	25.63	107.03
Digital	NA	NA	NA	NA	NA	NA
Electronics	96.07	16.34	112.41	410.68	161.71	572.39
Energy - Renewables	895.86	156.44	1052.30	381.09	55.7	436.79
Energy – Intensive Industries	223.62	132.30	355.92	174.01	134.37	308.38
Health	210.07	34.83	244.90	1059.49	238.68	1298.17
Mobility-Transport-Automotive	471.12	64.61	535.72	613.91	52.43	666.35
Proximity, Social Economy and Civil Security	NA	NA	NA	NA	NA	NA
Retail	NA	NA	NA	NA	NA	NA
Textile	136.85	164.33	301.18	126.34	88.60	214.94

Fig. 6.8 EU R&D funding on digital and green transitions, per industrial ecosystem (million EUR). Source: European Commission (2023). EMI Data Package Agri-Food.xlsx (live.com)

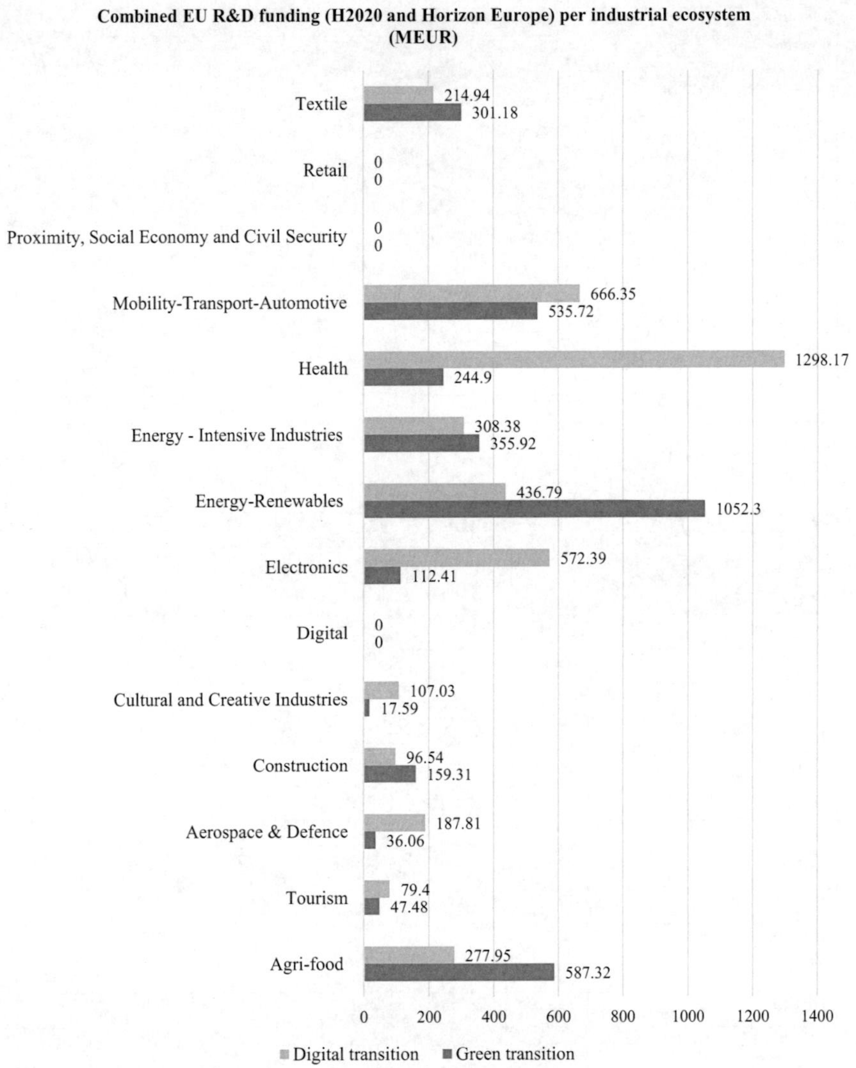

Fig. 6.9 Combined EU R&D funding (Horizon 2020 and Horizon Europe) on digital and green transitions, per industrial ecosystem (million EUR). Source: own elaboration based European Commission (2023). EMI Data Package Agri-Food.xlsx (live.com)

- *The research intensities of the respective ecosystems*: the ecosystems with higher R&D intensity (see the OECD 2016 classification of economic activities[7]) attract more R&I projects:
  - *High, medium-high and medium-R&D intensity ecosystems* (Aerospace and defence, Digital, Electronics, Health, Energy-Renewables and Energy-Intensive industries, Transport-Automotive-Mobility)
  - *Medium-low R&D intensity ecosystems* (Textile)
  - *Low R&D intensity ecosystems* (Agrifood, Tourism, Construction, Retail, and Cultural and Creative Industries). The Agrifood ecosystem with its large numbers of R&I projects is an exception here. Although it is considered as a (medium)/low-R&D intensity sector, it attracted higher R&I projects and EU R&D funding due to the interdisciplinary nature of the projects implemented in this sector, which include elements from other research-intensive sectors, especially Digital, Electronics and Health.[8]
- *A self-selection due to the structure and the approach of the two funding instruments*. As mentioned earlier, the Horizon 2020 European Green Deal Call was designed to finance projects with a strong technology 'impact' (technology development and demonstration, pilots, scalable innovative products and experiments). As these come primarily from sectors with high- and medium-R&D intensity, it is not surprising to see higher numbers of such projects across the respective industrial ecosystems. Horizon 2020 European Green Deal Call also targeted projects with a strong 'social' focus (governance, culture and behaviour, social innovation, civil society engagement and sustainability), which are well represented in the 'Knowledge and Citizens' projects. The European Partnerships of Horizon Europe reflect the thematic clusters of Pillar II 'Global Challenges and European Industrial Competitiveness'—Cluster 1: Health; Cluster 4: Digital, industry and space; Cluster 5: Climate, energy and mobility; and Cluster 6: Food, bioeconomy, natural resources, agriculture and environment—that are all sectors with high R&D intensity. The social dimension is not much visible in Pillar II, as it is addressed in Pillar III 'EIT', which was not included in the analysis.

---

[7] https://www.oecd-ilibrary.org/docserver/5jlv73sqqp8r-en.pdf?expires=1698516467&id=id&accname=guest&checksum=560B0D31C0514556D594621B977C2998

[8] For example, the H2020 partnerships NeoGiANT that develops novel natural antimicrobial products for the control and prevention of diseases in animal production using advanced isolation techniques; SISTERS that develops technological innovations in packaging for processors and retailers; and ZeroW that develops commercial, digital tools and instruments to reduce food waste. Also, among the Horizon Europe Partnerships (EPs), the EP for Agriculture of Data combines geospatial and Earth observation datasets to support sustainable agriculture in the EU; the EP Accelerating farming systems transition: agroecology living labs and research infrastructure develops a network of living labs and research infrastructures accelerating the transition towards agroecology in Europe; and the EP for a Circular bio-based Europe develops technologies for sourcing and conversion of biomass into bio-based products focusing on multiscale biorefinery processing.

- *Differences in the absorptive capacities of the industrial ecosystems* that are spread over various EU countries and regions, with different innovation assets and performances.

Contributions to the Knowledge Development Function of the Single Market

The R&I projects and the EU R&D funding discussed above contribute to the Knowledge Development function of the Single Market in several ways:

- *They cover a wide range of knowledge and technology areas and generate extensive knowledge outcomes*: Both types of R&I projects—from the Horizon 2020 European Green Deal call and from the Horizon Europe European Partnerships—cover a broad range of knowledge and technology areas (Table 6.3). They also produce extensive knowledge outcomes, e.g. new techniques and technological solutions, models, methodologies, customised support service and user-oriented services, reports, case studies, scientific papers, policy briefs, tools and toolkits, indicators, portals, peer-to-peer mentorship, conferences, brokerage events, etc.

- *They contribute to education, training and skills activities*: In addition to their R&I focus, several projects, especially among the European Partnerships of Horizon Europe, have developed education, training and skills activities for both industry and non-industry professionals, thus integrating education and skills formation into their R&I framework (Box 6.1).

Box 6.1 Education, Training and Skills Development Activities in European Partnerships

- *The European Partnership Photonics*[9] supports various projects that provide education and training for advanced skills in photonics for professionals and value chain partners. One of the projects undertaken in this framework is *PHABLABS 4.0* which trains photonics workforce for the rapidly expanding ecosystem of European Fab Labs and Makerslabs. Another one is *Photonics4All* that received EU funding to train all people and organisations engaged in photonics outreach.

(continued)

[9] https://www.photonics21.org/ppp-services/photonics-for-university.php

Box 6.1 (continued)

- *The European Partnership Built4People (B4P)* trains workforce and other actors in the built environment value chain and provides tools for training and certification. *NEBULA*[10] is one of the projects launched within B4P to establish a network of Innovation Clusters across Europe and connect innovators along the wider value chain. NEBULA organises a series of six webinars entitled 'New Bauhaus Stories' for peer learning to share experiences and insights about the New European Bauhaus.
- *The Clean Hydrogen Partnership*[11] includes activities that promote education and skills to ensure a qualified workforce for hydrogen technology advancements. Educational modules and training aimed to build expertise in the field include *NET-Tools (Novel Education and Training Tools)*[12] based on digital applications related to hydrogen and fuel cell technology and the *European Hydrogen Train the Trainer Programme for Responders*[13] that develops a sustainable trainer programme for a pan-European network of responder trainers in hydrogen safety, supporting the commercialisation of hydrogen and fuel cell technologies.
- *The Circular Bio-based Europe Joint Undertaking (CBE JU)* promotes advancements in the bio-based economy and supports education and training activities through the *BIOBec project*[14,15] for establishing six regional Bio-Based Education Centres (BBECs). The centres cover the Northern European region (Denmark, Finland, Germany, Ireland), the Mediterranean region (Italy, Spain, Greece and Portugal) and the Central and Eastern Europe region (Poland, Czechia and Bulgaria). The centres ensure wide geographical coverage in Europe and address different topics linked to various value chains, contributing to different regional ecosystems and closing the industry's skills and competence gaps.

Source: own elaboration

These activities are taking place in several industrial ecosystems and are particularly valuable in ecosystems such as Electronics, Construction, Energy-Intensive industries and Energy-Renewables that have been identified in the EMI Industrial Ecosystems reports to have a generally low level of green and digital skills in their workforce (Table 6.4).

[10] https://built4people.eu/nebula_project/

[11] https://www.clean-hydrogen.europa.eu/about-us/who-we-are_en

[12] https://www.clean-hydrogen.europa.eu/system/files/2021-12/3.NET-Tools_Peter%20Holtappels.pdf

[13] https://www.clean-hydrogen.europa.eu/projects-dashboard/projects-repository/hyresponder_en

[14] https://www.cbe.europa.eu/achievements/new-educational-model-drive-forward-europes-bioeconomy

[15] https://www.cbe.europa.eu/projects/biobec

Table 6.3 Knowledge and technology areas covered by the R&I projects

Horizon 2020 European Green Deal call	Horizon Europe European Partnerships
• *Clean Energy* (16 projects): energy decarbonisation through the development and deployment of innovative technologies, in particular large-scale hydrogen production, conversion of CO2 emissions from industrial processes into synthetic fuels, development of land-based renewable energy technologies and offshore renewable energy innovations. • *Climate change and biodiversity* (17 projects): mitigation and adaptation to climate change and the preservation of biodiversity, in particular prevention and management of wildfires, preservation and restoration of biodiversity in natural ecosystems, including coastal, water landscapes and forests; climate change adaptation and mitigation (with a highlight on urban areas) • *Food and health* (15 projects): reshaping the food and health sectors to better support the green transition, by reducing chemical and industrial pollution; circular value chains in the agrifood sector; innovative practices that support the farm to fork strategy • *Urban environment and mobility* (nine projects): green transition at the urban/local level, in particular multimodal connection and transport nodes, sustainable solutions for maritime and inland ports and airports, energy and resource efficiency in the built environment (buildings and neighbourhoods), and support to climate ambitions in cities • *Knowledge and citizens* (16 projects): behavioural change of citizens in the implementation of the European Green Deal, inclusion and empowerment of citizens to reduce GHG emissions and air pollution in and around cities, education and civic engagement enabling citizens to act on climate change, social and cultural change for the Green Deal	• *Cluster 1: Health* (9 projects)—technologies tackling infectious and rare diseases, antimicrobial resistance and pandemic preparedness; diagnostics, treatments and vaccines against reemerging epidemics; risk assessment of toxic chemicals; personalised medicine; national/regional healthcare systems • *Cluster 4: Digital, industry and space* (10 projects)—supercomputing, quantum computing, service and data infrastructure; electronics and photonics; smart networks and services, 5G cybersecurity toolbox and technology capacities for 6G systems; AI, data and robotics; clean steel-low-carbon steelmaking; metrology, manufacturing ecosystems for circular industries • *Cluster 5: Climate, energy and mobility* (11 projects)—digital and automation technologies for rail systems; digital technologies for air traffic management, air-ground integration and automation, airspace management and safe integration of drones; new aircraft technologies for clean aviation; clean hydrogen technologies; technologies for zero emission and competitive long distance heavy-duty vehicles; connected, cooperative and automated mobility (CCAM) technologies and services; technologies for zero-emission waterborne transport, batteries, urban transformative transitions and clean energy transitions • *Cluster 6: Food, bioeconomy, natural resources, agriculture and environment* (8 projects)—accelerating farming systems transition, i.e. agroecology living labs and research infrastructure; animal health and welfare; geospatial and Earth observation datasets for agriculture; biodiversity monitoring; knowledge-based solutions and innovative governance models for blue economy; safe and sustainable food systems; sourcing and conversion of biomass into bio-based products and circular economy; water security

Source: Selected from Green Deal Projects Working Groups I Research and Innovation (europa.eu) and European Partnerships in Horizon Europe (europa.eu)

Table 6.4 Professionals with digital and green transition skills employed in industrial ecosystems (share in total professionals). Data extracted from LinkedIn; Dataset: LinkedIn; Last updated: Jun 2023

Twin transition	Agrifood	Tourism	Aerospace and defence	Construction	Cultural and creative industries	Electronics	Energy-intensive industries	Health	Mobility, transportation and automotive	Social economy	Textiles
Advanced digital skills	0.02	0.02	0.18	0.06	0.05	0.14	0.05	0.04	0.08	0.04	0.03
Moderate digital skills	0.14	0.02	0.29	0.21	0.31	0.28	0.19	0.13	0.19	0.20	0.18
Green skills	0.03	0.15	0.06	0.07	0.03	0.05	0.06	0.02	0.04	0.05	0.02

Source: European Commission (2023). EMI Data Package Aerospace and Defence.xlsx (live.com). Worksheet 'Skills_supply'

6.2 Implications for the Industrial Ecosystems with Low Numbers of R&I Projects and EU Funding

One aspect that deserves attention is the low number or even absence of R&I projects and EU R&D funding in areas related to the green and digital transition in the ecosystems Retail, Textile, Tourism and Cultural and Creative Industries, which may affect their economic performance and capacity to implement green and digital technologies in the longer run. The impact of lower investment flows in these ecosystems is compensated to some extent by the indirect benefits derived from the economic links and overlaps with the ecosystems that have more R&I partnerships and funding (particularly Digital/Electronics, Energy-Renewables and Energy-Intensive industries and Mobility-Transport-Automotive). Benefits could include, for instance, greening of tourism services that may be enabled by investments in renewable energy and sustainable water management, digital advancements in the textile industry from digital market places and virtual trade shows, acceleration of high-value smart textile and digitalised manufacturing by using robotics and AI, etc. Also, the Recovery and Resilience Plans (RRP) provided some compensation for the lower levels of R&I investment in these ecosystems. For example, 15 RRPs have tourism-dedicated and tourism-related measures to upgrade tourism infrastructures and facilities and increase the supply of high-quality and sustainable tourism products and services, investing a total of EUR 11.35bn (2.6% of total RRF funding) in the tourism ecosystem and services.[16]

The lower investment flows can be an additional disadvantage for these ecosystems that have already been hard hit by the pandemic (European Commission, 2021a) and also have lower investment plans to tackle the climate change impact (European Commission, 2022c), as shown in Fig. 6.10.

These findings are confirmed by recent evidence provided by the European Monitor of Industrial Ecosystems (European Commission, 2023) in the individual analytical reports for each industrial ecosystem. For instance, in the Retail ecosystem, the green transition is identified to be still in an early stage, despite a dynamic uptake of environmentally sustainable practices. Only 26% of the SMEs surveyed in the EMI study have increased their investments in green technologies and environmental sustainability actions over the past 5 years, while a substantial 42% of the SMEs allocated less than 5% of their overall turnover for eco-friendly technologies and practices. Only 14% of retail SMEs used energy-saving technologies and 12.1% used recycled materials, while only 10% reported investments in recycling technologies within their company. Renewable energy technologies have been taken up by 9% of the respondents. Advanced technologies like hydrogen utilisation and carbon capture are among the least adopted by the respondents.[17] A similar situation was

[16] https://single-market-economy.ec.europa.eu/industry/strategy/ecosystems_en. See Fiche 'Tourism'.

[17] Analytical report *Monitoring the twin transition of industrial ecosystems*—RETAIL. https://monitor-industrial-ecosystems.ec.europa.eu/industrial-ecosystems/retail

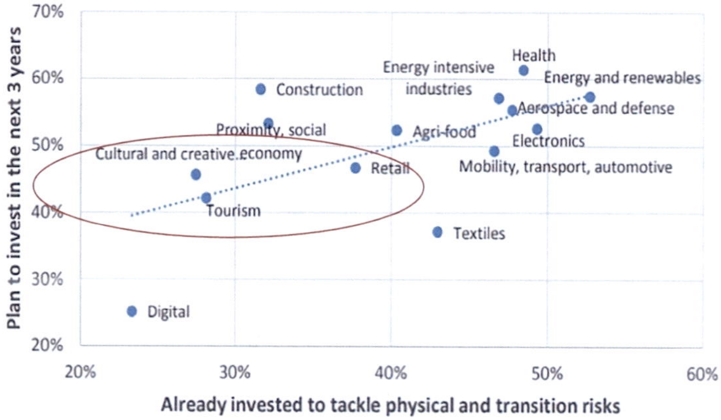

Source: EIB Investment Survey (wave 2021).
Question: Now thinking about investments to tackle the impacts of weather events and to deal with the process of reduction in carbon emissions, which of the following applies?

Fig. 6.10 Investment plans to tackle climate change impact, by industrial ecosystem. Source: European Commission (2022c), p. 33

identified also in the Textile ecosystem, where, despite some positive developments, real commitments to environmentally sustainable business practices are still limited and the share of green activities within the overall business operation is still low (e.g. 32% of the textile SMEs use recycled materials, only 23.3% of them use bio-based sustainable materials and less than 5% use recycled materials for their products).[18] In the Tourism ecosystem, 44% of the EMI-surveyed SMEs increased investments for the green transition and environmental sustainability during the past 5 years, while 30.6% adopted recycled materials and 21% adopted advanced bio-based/organic materials. Only 28% invested in energy-saving technologies and 26% adopted solutions to reduce food waste.[19]

These ecosystems are also among those where SMEs contribute most to international value chains—more than 50% of value added (European Commission, 2023a). Potential consequences of the lower R&I investments in these ecosystems may involve losses of competitiveness and performance of SMEs in cross-border supply chains, where they may supply larger players within the ecosystem, even when they are not exporting themselves (Fig. 6.11).

[18] Analytical report *Monitoring the twin transition of industrial ecosystems*—TEXTILES. https://monitor-industrial-ecosystems.ec.europa.eu/industrial-ecosystems/textiles

[19] Analytical report *Monitoring the twin transition of industrial ecosystems*—TOURISM. https://monitor-industrial-ecosystems.ec.europa.eu/industrial-ecosystems/tourism

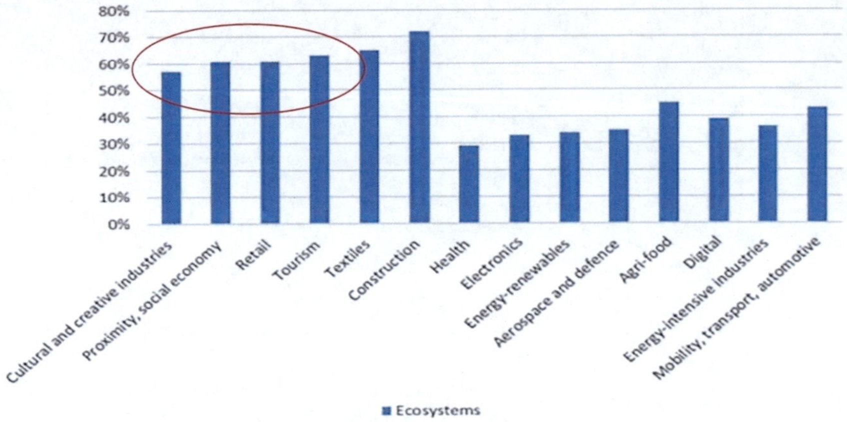

Fig. 6.11 SMEs' contribution per industrial ecosystem (in value added). Source: European Commission (2023a), p. 12

6.3 Function: Knowledge Diffusion/Exchange Through Networks

The main factors contributing to this function are the structure and the collaboration activities developed within the consortia and networks created by the R&I projects funded under the European Green Deal call of Horizon 2020 and the European Partnerships of Horizon Europe. The structure of these consortia and networks follows a Quadruple Helix format (university-industry-government-civil society stakeholders) with large numbers of professional public and private organisations from one or more industrial sectors and a broad regional and national geographical spread in Europe. Evidence in this regard comes from the several evaluation reports of these projects that are discussed below.

R&I Projects Under Horizon 2020 European Green Deal Call

Relevant insights regarding the contribution of these projects to the Knowledge diffusion/exchange through networks function come from an evaluation of the response to the call (European Commission, 2021b) that highlights several relevant aspects:

- *The project consortia have a broad international participation from EU countries, Associated Countries as well as Third countries:* 1778 successful participants selected from 75 countries. EU countries accounted for 90% of the successful participants and of the EU requested contribution in the successful proposals, with Spain, Italy, Germany, the Netherlands, Belgium and France

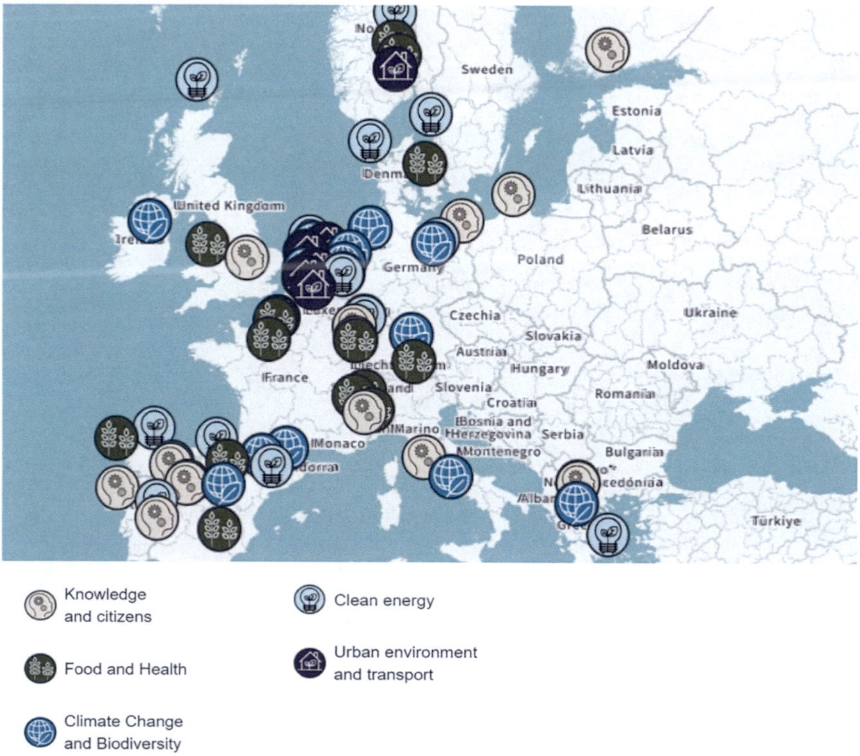

Fig. 6.12 International coverage of projects under Horizon 2020 European Green Deal call. Source: Interactive projects map. https://projects.research-and-innovation.ec.europa.eu/en/strategy/strategy-2020-2024/environment-and-climate/european-green-deal/green-deal-projects-support/green-deal-projects-interactive-map/map

topping both lists (p. 7). Most projects are concentrated in Western, Northern and Southern Europe, with a limited representation of Central and Eastern Europe countries (Fig. 6.12).

- *The project consortia involve large and dense collaboration networks of public and private institutions of various types:* over 26,000 collaborations between universities, research and technology centres, companies (SMEs and large companies), clusters, government authorities and other public bodies, civil society, non-governmental organisations, etc. The private sector has the largest participation (more than 40% of the applicants, of which about half are SMEs), followed by research and technology organisations (25%), higher education establishments (19%), public bodies (7%) and "other"—civil society, non-governmental organisations, international organisations, associations, etc. (approx. 10%). The high number of applications from the private sector was attributed to the Green Deal call focus on mature technological solutions and innovation and demonstration actions, while public bodies' applications seemed to focus more on the demonstration and pilot activities in several topics. The densest collaborations are

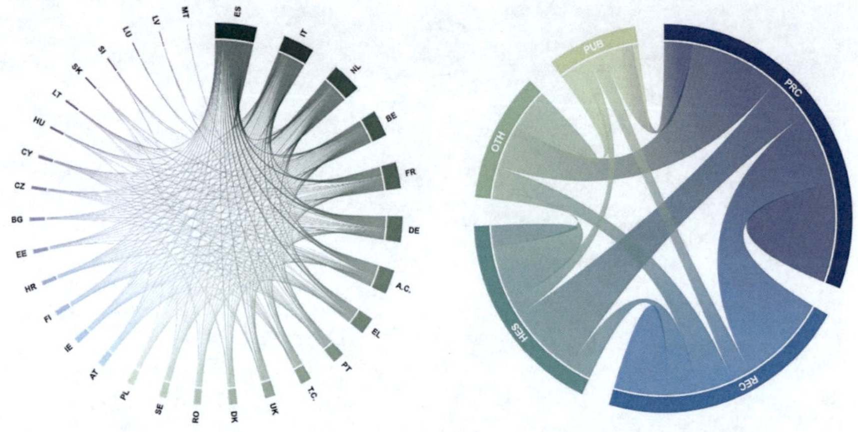

Associated (A.C.) and Third (T.C) Countries are grouped.

PRC: Private for-profit entities (excl. Higher or Secondary Education Establishments).

REC: Research and Technology Organisations.

HES: Higher or Secondary Education Establishments.

PUB: Public bodies (excl. Research Organisations & Secondary or Higher Education Establishments).

OTH: Others

Fig. 6.13 Collaboration between countries and between different types of participants in the projects under Horizon 2020 European Green Deal call. Source: European Commission (2021b), p. 9 and p. 17

between private for-profit entities (excl. higher or secondary education establishments) and the research and technology organisations (Fig. 6.13).

R&I Projects Under the Horizon Europe European Partnerships

The evaluation of Horizon Europe European Partnerships presented in the Biennial Monitoring Report 2022 (European Commission, 2022) shows that most partnerships include various types of stakeholders in collaborative activities. In most cases, these activities consist of stakeholder fora, open events, open calls, activities in new countries, external networks, communication plans, technical workshops, mini-conferences and publications. Such activities have been reported in all projects in Clusters 1, 4 and 5 (p. 76). Some differences were observed in the strategy adopted by the different types of partnerships in involving stakeholders (p. 77):

(i) Co-funded partnerships tended to increase synergies and cooperation especially with national and regional authorities and Member States and favoured the

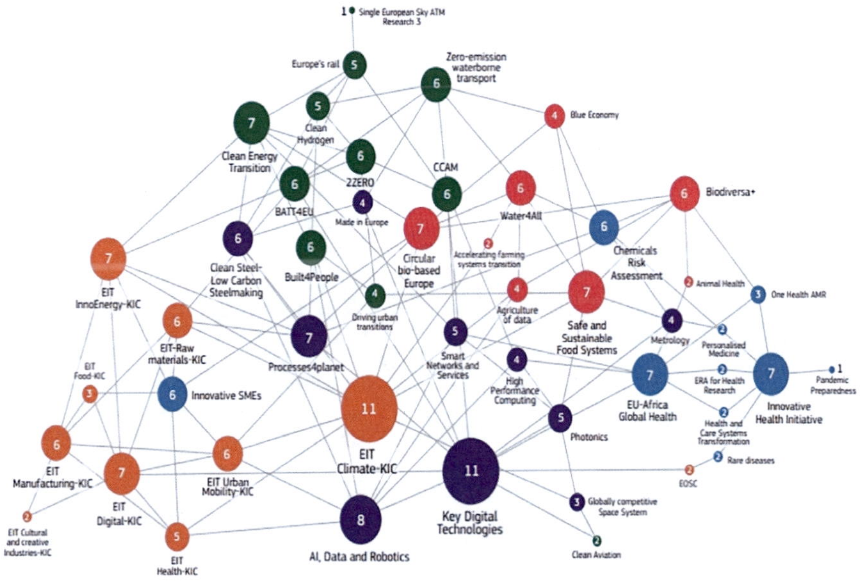

*Source: common indicators survey, November 2021. Cluster 1 – **blue**, Cluster 4 – **violet**, Cluster 5 – **green**, Cluster 6 – **red**, Cross-pillar – **orange***

Fig. 6.14 Collaboration activities between the Horizon Europe European Partnerships. Source: European Commission (2022), p. 8

involvement of stakeholders and new partners, especially SMEs, through more co-creation and collaborations.

(ii) Co-programmed partnerships tended to involve stakeholders mainly in workshops, hubs, platforms, plenary meetings and stakeholder fora and developed additional communication activities to address diverse challenges, such as fragmentation, complexity and scarce resources.

(iii) Institutionalised partnerships tended to increase their stakeholder involvement through stakeholder fora, open calls and enhanced communication activities.

The evaluation identified strong collaboration and synergies between the European Partnerships of Pillar II—Clusters 1, 4, 5 and 6—and the EIT projects of Pillar III in cross-cutting topics like climate and digital issues. The EIT Climate-KIC and some Cluster 4 projects, such as Key Digital Technologies and AI, Data and Robotics, stand out with the largest number of planned coordinated and joint activities with other partnerships (Fig. 6.14), indicating good synergies and coherence between the European Partnerships and across different clusters.

These networks also demonstrate a commitment to improving openness, by including newcomer partners mostly from widening countries in Europe, especially Romania, Hungary, Bulgaria, Latvia and Luxembourg (Fig. 6.15). Besides newcomer countries, the European Partnerships have also broadened the range of actors involved across the value chain—either as direct members or in the governance

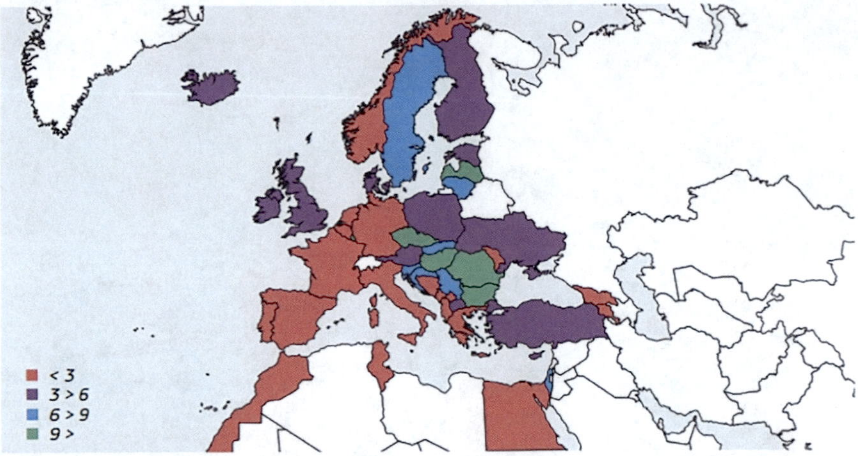

Source: Common indicators survey.

Fig. 6.15 Geographical coverage of targeted newcomer partners. European Commission (2022), p. 8

processes. For example, the Smart Networks and Services JU has expanded its membership to include communities from the Internet of Things and cloud domain (European Commission, 2022, p. 81).

The collaboration among the networks created by the European Partnerships has also been enhanced by the *Inter-Partnership Assembly*, launched in December 2020 by the European Commission to align the multi-annual work programmes of the different Partnerships (and other collaborative parts in Horizon Europe) and stimulate synergies between them. The Assembly encouraged the development of research/innovation topics that can be addressed by different European Partnerships, initially in Cluster 5 and later between Cluster 4 and 5 (Box 6.2), particularly those dealing with hydrogen, electrification, manufacturing and IT technologies that are common enabling technologies serving all the other industrial sectors and driving climate-neutral technologies in multiple industrial sectors.

Box 6.2 Synergies Between European Partnerships: The Inter-Partnership Assembly

The Inter-Partnership Assembly had initially focused on synergies between Cluster 5 Partnerships (to link the use of hydrogen technologies with applications), but later the focus expanded to include also Cluster 4.

Examples include the following:

- Electrification technologies (2Zero, Rail, Waterborne, Clean Aviation, … and Batt4EU)

(continued)

Box 6.2 (continued)

- Cities and built environment: CETP (Co-Fund on Clean Energy Transition), DUT (Co-fund on Driving Urban Transition), CCAM, B4P (co-programmed PP on building environment) and Cities Mission
- Digital technologies (e.g. HPC, SNS, KDT, artificial intelligence and photonics and other sectoral Partnerships in energy, transport, health, construction, agriculture, etc.)
- Manufacturing/process technologies (made in Europe/European Metrology/ P4Planet and other sectoral Partnerships in energy, transport, health, construction, agriculture, etc.)

Source: European Commission (2022), p. 85

The Joint Undertakings (JUs)

A particular type of projects among the European Partnerships that have very large consortia and networks are the *Joint Undertakings (JUs)*. These have been set up by the European Commission to complement the Horizon Europe framework by addressing global challenges and priorities that require critical mass and long-term vision.[20] The JUs are partnerships of the *institutionalised* type (based on Article 171 of the Treaty establishing the European Community, now Article 187 of the TFEU) with the distinct mission to address global challenges and priorities, contribute to related EU policies, enable large joint investment by public and private actors and execute EU research, technological development and demonstration programmes.

Eleven JUs have been established to date as public-private partnerships involving the European Union, represented by the European Commission, governments of the EU Member States and of some non-EU countries and industry. They focus on aeronautics, medicines, fuel cells and hydrogen, nanoelectronics and embedded computing systems and are spread across the Pillar II Clusters 1, 4, 5 and 6 (Box 6.3).

Box 6.3 Joint Undertakings with Large Consortia and Networks

- *Innovative Health Initiative (IHI)*[21] *(Cluster 1):* this is a partnership for health R&I between the EU and Europe's life science industries. Partners:

(continued)

[20] https://eur-lex.europa.eu/EN/legal-content/summary/public-private-partnerships-under-horizon-europe.html

[21] https://european-union.europa.eu/institutions-law-budget/institutions-and-bodies/search-all-eu-institutions-and-bodies/innovative-health-initiative-joint-undertaking-ihi-ju_en

Box 6.3 (continued)

the European Union, represented by the European Commission, and the European life science industry, represented by the industry associations COCIR, EFPIA (including Vaccines Europe), EuropaBio and MedTech Europe.

- *Global Health EDCTP3*[22] *(Cluster 1):* this is a partnership for clinical development of new or improved health technologies for infectious diseases, including (re-)emerging diseases. Partners: the European Union, represented by the European Commission, and the European and Developing Countries Clinical Trials Partnership (EDCTP) Association, representing the governments of European and sub-Saharan African countries participating in the partnership.
- *Key Digital Technologies*[23] *(Cluster 4):* this is a partnership for the development of processors and semiconductor technologies. In 2023 it was replaced by a successor—the *Chips JU*[24]—which develops advanced nanoelectronic chip technologies and systems manufactured in Europe. Partners: the European Union, represented by the European Commission, the 27 EU Member States, non-EU states (such as Israel, Norway and Türkiye) and industrial associations representing the micro- and nanoelectronics, smart integrated systems and embedded/cyber-physical systems sectors (AENEAS, EPoSS and INSIDE).
- *Smart Networks and Services (SNS JU)*[25] *(Cluster 4)*: this is a partnership that aims to ensure Europe's technology sovereignty in 6G and deployment of 5G. Partners: the European Union, represented by the European Commission and the 6G Smart Networks and Services Industry Association—6GIA.
- *High Performance Computing (EuroHPC)*[26] *(Cluster 4)*: this partnership aims to make Europe a world leader in supercomputing and support the digital transformation of its economy while ensuring its technological sovereignty. EuroHPC implements a hyper-connected supercomputing, quantum computing and service and data infrastructure ecosystem for a network of HPC competence centres serving large industry users and SMEs, researchers, public administrations and industry across Europe.

(continued)

[22] https://globalhealth-edctp3.eu/

[23] https://digital-strategy.ec.europa.eu/en/news/key-digital-technologies-new-partnership-help-speed-transition-green-and-digital-europe

[24] https://european-union.europa.eu/institutions-law-budget/institutions-and-bodies/search-all-eu-institutions-and-bodies/chips-joint-undertaking_en

[25] https://digital-strategy.ec.europa.eu/en/policies/smart-networks-and-services-joint-undertaking

[26] https://eurohpc-ju.europa.eu/index_en

Box 6.3 (continued)

Partners: the European Union, represented by the European Commission, the 27 EU Member States and non-EU countries (such as Israel, Montenegro, North Macedonia, Norway, Serbia, Türkiye and the UK). Private members: the European Technology Platform for High Performance Computing (ETP4HPC), the Big Data Value Association (BDVA) and the European Quantum Industry Consortium (QuIC).

- *European partnership on metrology*[27] *(Cluster 4)*: this partnership relies on the Regional Metrology Organisation of Europe (EURAMET), which coordinates the cooperation of National Metrology Institutes and Designated Institutes in Europe in fields such as research in metrology, traceability of measurements to the SI units, international recognition of national measurement standards and related Calibration and Measurement Capabilities. EURAMET facilitates the development of the national metrology infrastructures and coordinates 12 European Metrology Networks that analyse the European and global metrology needs and formulate common metrology strategies for research, infrastructure, knowledge transfer and services.[28]
- *Clean Hydrogen*[29] *(Cluster 5)*: this partnership supports R&I on hydrogen technologies in Europe. Partners: the European Union, represented by the European Commission, the fuel cell and hydrogen industries represented by Hydrogen Europe and the research community represented by Hydrogen Europe Research. The R&I activities of the Clean Hydrogen JU are guided largely by *EU's Hydrogen Strategy* and the policy developments in this context, contributing to its implementation.
- *Clean Aviation*[30]*:* this partnership develops the next generation of ultraefficient low-carbon aircraft technologies, with novel (hybrid) electrical power sources, engines and systems. The Clean Aviation programme is built on three key thrusts, each with targeted R&I and demonstration efforts:
  - Hybrid electric regional aircraft, with electrical power architectures and maturing technologies for demonstration of novel configurations, on-board energy concepts and flight control
  - Ultraefficient short and short-medium range aircraft with innovative aircraft architectures essential for the transition to low/zero-emission energy sources

(continued)

[27] https://www.euramet.org/research-innovation/metrology-partnership/

[28] https://www.euramet.org/european-metrology-networks

[29] https://www.clean-hydrogen.europa.eu/index_en

[30] https://www.clean-aviation.eu/

Box 6.3 (continued)

– Disruptive technologies to enable hydrogen-powered aircraft as an alternative zero-carbon fuel

- *Single European Sky ATM Research*[31] *(SESAR) (Cluster 5):* this partnership serves the modernisation of Europe's air and ground Air Traffic Management (ATM) infrastructure and operational procedures and implementation of ATM Master Plan. Partners: the EU, represented by the European Commission, EUROCONTROL and a wide range of public and private, civil and military aviation stakeholders.
- *Europe's Rail*[32] *(Cluster 5):* this partnership delivers a high-capacity integrated European railway network by eliminating barriers to interoperability and providing solutions for full integration, covering traffic management, vehicles, infrastructure and services, with faster uptake and deployment of projects and innovations. Partners: the EU, represented by the European Commission, several national rail infrastructure authorities of the EU Member States, companies and research centres in the rail area, etc.
- *Circular Bio-based Europe*[33] *(Cluster 6):* this partnership aims to advance competitive circular bio-based industries in Europe. Partners: the European Union, represented by the European Commission, and the Bio-based Industries Consortium (BIC) that includes representatives of several sectors, such as agriculture and agrifood, aquaculture and marine, chemicals and materials (including bioplastics), forestry, pulp and paper and technology providers and waste management and treatment. BIC also has associate members such as research organisations, academia and trade associations.

Source: own elaboration

A recent evaluation of Horizon 2020 (European Commission, 2024) highlighted the success of the Fuel Cells and Hydrogen JU in attracting some of the major industrial players, significantly consolidating a previously fragmented hydrogen ecosystem. Similarly, the Bio-based Industries JU had a structuring effect, effectively organising value chains across various sectors and mobilising key stakeholders across different regions. Additionally, the European Metrology Programme for Innovation and Research facilitated collaboration among national metrology institutions, reducing fragmentation and duplication and strengthening the EU's position as a global leader in metrology research. All these achievements demonstrate notable contributions to the function of Knowledge diffusion/exchange through networks.

[31] https://transport.ec.europa.eu/transport-modes/air/single-european-sky/sesar-project_en

[32] https://rail-research.europa.eu/about-europes-rail/europes-rail-mission-and-objectives/

[33] https://biconsortium.eu/about

6.4 Market Formation/Entrepreneurial Activity

In this section, the two functions are addressed together, as they are closely related.

Contribution to Market Formation

A primary contribution to market formation of the R&I projects financed both under the Horizon 2020 European Green Deal call and the Horizon Europe European Partnerships is the wide range of testing and experimentation activities, demonstration of technical solutions, transformation of ideas into pilot applications, validation and upscaling through a variety of Living Labs, trials and pilots, City Hubs, large-scale demonstrators, etc. (Table 6.5). Both programmes have this focus 'by design', as the activities for technology development, demonstration and scalable innovative products have been an eligibility criterion in both calls. These activities aim to create market interest, identify niche markets and develop specialized products, creating demand and attracting financial support for emerging technologies. They can also contribute to the development and integration of new environmental standards.

Participation in consortium activities can facilitate data sharing, which can lead to data-driven products and services for new or existing markets. The connections that SMEs and start-ups can develop with other partners and stakeholders both nationally and internationally can lead to new business opportunities, introduce innovations to a broader customer base and allow European innovations to access global markets. Moreover, as many of these technologies are new or disruptive and are associated with strategic industries in Europe, they support the EU's competitiveness and technical sovereignty. This contribution is particularly notable in the case of several European Partnerships under Horizon Europe (Table 6.6) that lead in technological performance, facilitating 'learning curves' both for the producers and the users.

All these market formation activities are highly relevant considering the 'European paradox'—the perceived failure of European countries to translate scientific advances into marketable innovations. This has been recognised as a weakness of the European R&I systems for several decades and has been at the centre of numerous policy debates and recommendations to reduce the effect (e.g. Dosi et al., 2006 recommend less emphasis on 'networking' and more on policy measures for strengthening both frontier research and corporate actors in the relatively weak European industry).

Contribution to the Entrepreneurship Function

Both types of R&I projects support entrepreneurship by fostering an environment where innovative ideas can turn into viable businesses. The demonstration,

Table 6.5 Selected R&I projects that include experimentation and demonstration activities

Horizon 2020 European Green Deal Call	Horizon Europe European Partnerships
• ***Eleven** Living Labs* for an integrated management of extreme wildfire events in Europe (FIRE-RES) • Seven Living Labs to codevelop a framework for human-centred climate services (I-CISK) • Seven City Hubs to accelerate co-creation of services and upscaling, building on peer-to-peer learning and involvement of urban authorities, private sector, civil society (REACHOUT-Cities) • Nine Pilots to develop a systemic approach to coastal restoration (REST COAST) • Twelve large-scale demonstrators across Europe for forest restoration and adaptation (SUPERB) • Field testing and demonstration of digital and space-based technologies and agroecological and organic practices in an aquaponic plant and open-field vegetable farms (PestNu) • Action and Knowledge Sites for restoration upscaling and sharing best practice experience and knowledge (WaterLANDS) • 16 MW scalable and fast-cycling modules for building a 100 MW electrolyser (GreenH2 Atlantic) • Six large-scale demonstration projects of climate positive circular communities in six cities in Czech Republic, Denmark, Italy, Netherlands, Norway and Spain, showcasing over 50 innovations related to the construction and energy industries (ARV) • Citizen Science Lab—with a focus on women, young people and hard-to-reach groups to provide the skills to codesign and undertake environmental scientific experiments (COMPAIR) • Eight Living Labs and a participatory Environmental Impact Hub, to collect data about climate change and environmental hazards and make it available to citizens to understand how their own behaviour can affect climate change and how they can reduce their carbon and environmental footprint (ICHANGE)	• Large-scale demonstrators of low-carbon technologies (clean steel production) leading to a 50% reduction in CO2 emissions by 2030 and by 80–95% by 2050 in at least 12 areas funded by the partnership (Clean Steel Partnership) • Forty large-scale demonstration projects by 2025 and 60 by 2027 to produce clean hydrogen and distribution, storage and end-use applications of low-carbon hydrogen (Clean Hydrogen) • Several types of Integrated Technology Demonstrators (ITDs) and System Platform Demonstrations (SPD) aimed to improve market uptake of innovative railway solutions through large-scale demonstration activities (Europe's Rail) • Large-scale demonstrations of automated mobility systems and services within cities (Connected, Cooperative and Automated Mobility CCAM) • Pilots and full-scale trials to provide and validate enablers and solutions for full digitization of the European vertical industries in order to improve the business operation (Smart Networks and Services) • European Robotics Week—a citizen outreach event where academic laboratories and companies organize demonstrations, public hackathons, lectures and debates with the public (AI, data and robotics) • Demonstration and prototype projects covering TRL 5–7 scale (Photonics Partner ship) • Digital Innovation Hubs with demonstrators, pilot sites and field labs to test the digital transformation of manufacturing (digital platforms, AI, machine learning, simulation and modelling (digital twins), robust and secure industrial real-time communication technologies) and engage SMEs in the digital transformation (Made in Europe) • Hubs for Circularity (H4C) to catalyse regional industry-society collaboration by connecting various regional stakeholders to develop circularity and carbon neutrality, industrial-urban symbiosis and circularity (Processes 4Planet) • In-Orbit demonstration/validation for mature and disruptive space technologies

(continued)

Table 6.5 (continued)

Horizon 2020 European Green Deal Call	Horizon Europe European Partnerships
	(Globally competitive Space Systems) • Very Large-scale Demonstrations (VLD) of mature concepts and technologies (Autonomous operations, Airport infrastructure for New Vehicles) (Integrated Air Traffic Management) • 34+ flagship demonstrators, 106+ other demonstrators contributing to the flagship demonstrators, 1000+ technologies by the end of the programme (Clean Aviation)

Source: selected from Green Deal Projects Working Groups | Research and Innovation (europa.eu) and European Partnerships in Horizon Europe (europa.eu)

Table 6.6 Selected European Partnerships that develop new/disruptive technologies

Horizon Europe European Partnerships
• *Bio-Based Industry JU*: the EUCALIVA project funded in this JU extracted industrial polymers from lignin, an alternative that grows on trees. The SHERPACK project promote sustainable packaging to replace fossil-based plastic packaging with bio-based materials. The AgriMax project processes organic waste. The projects RECOVER, BIZENTE and ENZYCLE focus on microorganisms, enzymes, earthworms and insects to break down plastics, while the GRETE project develops new, non-toxic and recyclable solvents that will boost the safety and sustainability of making textiles from wood. • *Clean Sky JU:* introduced promising technologies with the Tech TP engine demonstrator that develops a 100% European-built, sustainable, low-fuel and low-noise engine for use in general aviation and smaller commuter-sized aircraft (up to 19 passengers). The UltraFan technology demonstrator introduced the next generation of environmentally friendly gas turbines for large commercial aircraft. The RACER demonstrator combines an innovative wing-box design with lighter structures and improved power management efficiency. The Dense project combines different types of sensors to make a self-driving car 'see' better than its driver in bad weather conditions; the ENSO project addressed the energy needs of small autonomous systems; and the SILENCE project dealt with some unique applications of ultrasound. • *EuroHPC JU* signed four contracts for petascale supercomputers to be hosted in Luxembourg, Czechia, Slovenia and Bulgaria, giving access to valuable computing resources in these countries. Two further contracts for precursor to exascale supercomputers were signed by the JU to be hosted in Italy and Finland. • *Fuel Cells and Hydrogen (FCH) JU* targets low-emission flight. A commercially viable fuel cell for zero-carbon emergency and in-flight power is developed in FLHYSAFE, while HEAVEN is designing compressed-fuel tanks and a high-power fuel cell for fully hydrogen planes. Other projects, such as H2ME and H2ME 2, develop many of the 150 sites of public hydrogen refuelling stations in operation in Europe, making it the largest network in the world. FCH JU projects are scaling up electrolysers that generate hydrogen from renewables and installing them in large refineries and factories. This technology is a viable alternative to hydrogen production from natural gas and contributes to decarbonising industries and businesses in emerging hydrogen valleys.

Source: selected from European Commission (2022), pp. 92–93

prototype building and experimentation, validation and upscaling activities discussed above contribute to entrepreneurial activities, as they may lead to market formation, new business opportunities, investors and potential customers. The start-ups, spin-offs and entrepreneurs that are often part of the R&I project consortia and networks have opportunities to collaborate with the other partners (businesses, universities and research institutions) and have access to research findings and innovation networks that may accelerate the formation of new business ventures or the growth of the existing ones. Knowledge and technology transfer between research institutions and industry partners, as well as business incubation and acceleration, help start-ups and SMEs bring their innovative ideas to the market and navigate the venture formation process. This can facilitate market entry and growth of start-ups, particularly in sectors with strict regulatory requirements, such as healthcare and aviation. Furthermore, the networking and matchmaking events that are organised by many R&I projects connect entrepreneurs with potential partners, customers and investors and create opportunities for entrepreneurs to showcase their innovations and build strategic relationships within the same sector or across sectors.

The European Partnerships provide some relevant examples of activities for SMEs and entrepreneurs (Box 6.4):

Box 6.4 Selected European Partnerships with Activities for SMEs and Entrepreneurs

- *BIOSWITCH: Encouraging Brand Owners to Switch-to-Bio-Based in highly innovative ecosystems*[34] (2020–2022) is a project established within the European Partnership *Circular Bio-based Europe Joint Undertaking (CBE JU)* to support bio-based SMEs with tailored coaching, funding opportunities and networking events. The project helped businesses switch from fossil-based to bio-based production processes, by creating a framework—through a series of events and outreach activities—that placed brand owners at the centre of a triangle consisting of the public administration, the bio-based industry and consumers. These interactions facilitated brand owners' efforts to identify solutions for reducing the potential risk in making this switch. The project also developed a BIOSWITCH Toolbox to assist companies in their transition.

  Source: https://www.cbe.europa.eu/projects/bioswitch

- *The Photonics Partnership* launched several European pilot lines to help companies take photonics technologies from lab into market. The companies can take their good ideas, scale them up and validate them with the first customers for commercial production. The pilot lines include thousands of

(continued)

[34] https://www.cbe.europa.eu/projects/bioswitch

Box 6.4 (continued)

high-tech SMEs in Europe who often lack access to advanced, cost-intensive infrastructures and expertise needed to manufacture new and innovative products. One of the pilot lines is *Photon Hub*, a unique pan-European initiative bringing together more than 500 photonics experts from 15 Member States and providing a full-service one-stop-shop Photonics Innovation Hub to support companies in photonics orienteering, training and reskilling, deep technology innovation support, business and investment coaching, as well as guidance to regional support. Furthermore, the Photonics partnership encouraged photonics start-ups to participate in the activities of the European Innovation Council and advised them of financing opportunities and actively promoted their participation in investment events. Access to venture capital for photonics start-ups and entrepreneurs was created by holding an annual European Photonics Venture Forum. The Photonics partnership also helps to generate potential leads for the EIB to invest in photonics, furthering access to capital for SMEs in the later growth phase.

Source: https://www.photonics21.org/ppp-projects/workgroup-7/PhotonHub.php and European Commission (2022a), p.80

6.5 Function: Resource Mobilisation

The large amounts of investment mobilised by the R&I projects from the EC, national budgets and the private sector and their multi-annual allocation exemplify this function.

The R&I projects financed under the European Green Deal call of Horizon 2020 (73 projects) received EUR 1 trillion from the EC (European Commission, 2021b). Among the five thematic Working Groups of these partnerships, Clean Energy received the highest allocation (EUR 492 million), followed by Urban Environment and Mobility (EUR 285 million) (Fig. 6.16).

The European Partnerships in Horizon Europe (49 projects) mobilised significant financial resources too: EUR 23.8 billion from the EC, EUR 9 billion from Member States and Associated Countries and EUR 22.4 billion from Industry (in total EUR 31.4 billion from partners other than the EU) (Fig. 6.17). These amounts account for 25% of the total Horizon Europe budget. Two-thirds (67%) of the collective resources of the European Partnerships support Green Deal projects, in a significant increase (38%) relative to the predecessor Horizon 2020 (European Commission, 2022, p. 6).

Cluster 4 ‘Digital, Industry and Space’ and Cluster 5 ‘Climate, Energy and Mobility’ received the largest amounts (Table 6.7).

Fig. 6.16 Overview of projects funded by Horizon 2020 European Green Deal call, by Working Group. Source: https://projects.research-and-innovation.ec.europa.eu/en/strategy/strategy-2020-2024/environment-and-climate/european-green-deal/green-deal-projects-support/green-deal-projects-working-groups

Table 6.7 Budget of the Horizon Europe European Partnerships (million EUR)

	EU contribution	Commitments from private partners	Commitment from public partners
Cluster 1: Health	2710	1439.88	711.37
Cluster 4: Digital, Industry and Space	8340	9151.16	5245.79
Cluster 5: Climate, Energy and Mobility	7190	10,740	886.2
Cluster 6: Food, Bioeconomy, Natural resources, Agriculture and Environment	2046	1000	960
Other pillars	3594	No data available (KICs)	1233.3

Source: Selected from European Commission (2022), pp. 219–223

6.6 Function: Guidance of the Search

This function is considered here in a broader sense of governance, policymaking and support to the development of specific industry trends, technologies, standards and certification processes. Considering the complex structure of the projects, several partners contribute to this function:

- *The European Commission* exerts an important role through the design and general management of the programmes (definition of eligibility rules, allocation of funding, evaluation, etc.), which have seen several elements of novelty (Box 6.5 and Fig. 6.17.
- *Public and private partners that constitute the project consortia and networks* in a Quadruple Helix format (scientific and business communities, government authorities, citizens and civil society): they perform various activities that result in setting industry trends, or influence policymaking at EU or national level by determining changes in existing regulations or policies, or accelerate the adoption of new policies, strategies, standards and certification processes, or encourage government support for specific industries or technologies. For instance, the

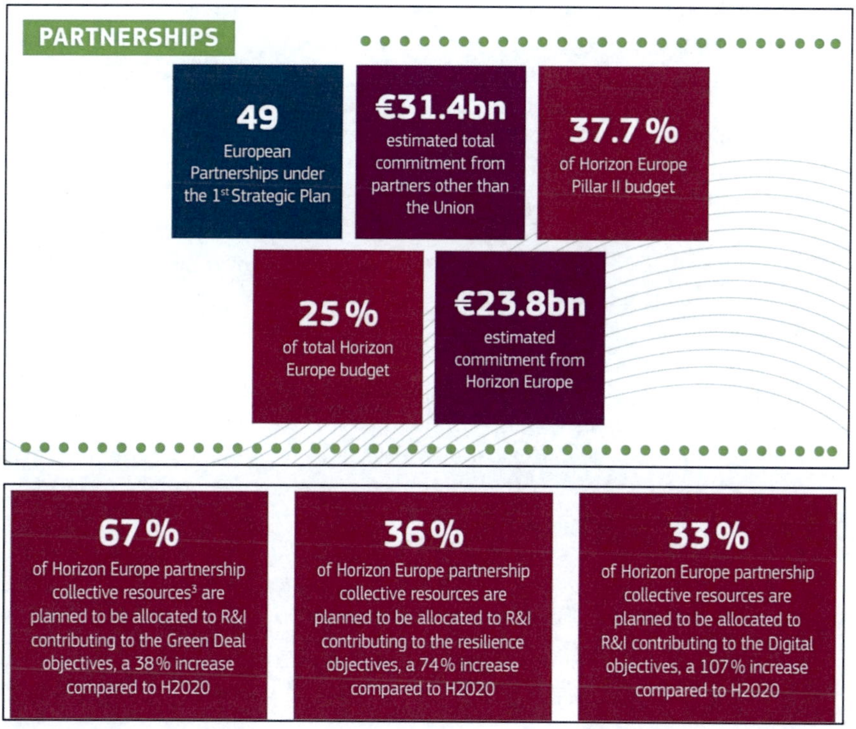

Fig. 6.17 Budget commitments to the European Partnerships under Horizon Europe. Source: European Commission (2022), pp. 6–7

partners of the *European Partnership Clean Aviation* contributed to policymaking and regulatory changes to promote the use of sustainable aviation fuels and low-emission aircraft to reduce aviation emissions. The *European Partnership on Clean Hydrogen* influenced the development of the European Hydrogen Strategy, which aims to promote hydrogen as a clean energy carrier through a set of regulatory and policy measures for hydrogen production, infrastructure development and market uptake. The *Key Digital Technologies European Partnership (KDT)* contributed to the EU's Digital Europe programme, which supports digital innovation and the creation of a regulatory framework for AI, ensuring responsible and ethical AI deployment. The *European Partnership on Metrology* advances regulations and standards for metrology initiatives (e.g. the work on quantum technologies aligns with the EU's efforts to develop standards for quantum technologies, shaping the regulatory landscape in this emerging field).

Box 6.5 Contribution of Horizon Europe European Partnerships to the Function Guidance of the Search: Novelties in Programme Design and Governance

- *Coherent criteria for all European Partnerships*: (i) directionality and additionality, (ii) coherence and synergies, (iii) transparency and openness, (iv) international visibility and (v) flexibility of implementation. Partners' objectives and long-term vision are agreed upon in Strategic Research and Innovation Agendas (SRIAs).
- *A more strategic and impact-oriented approach to EU priorities and stronger synergies with other initiatives at EU, national or local level,* based on a common vision, a critical mass of investments and joint activities agreed upon in the common SRIAs, a focus on more disruptive changes in European R&I systems and technological solutions, and an extended engagement of stakeholders.
- *A new Strategic Coordinating Process*, centred on a core *Partnership Knowledge Hub* that coordinates interactions and meetings between the stakeholders; an annual Partnership *Stakeholder Forum* that brings together the whole community for networking, sharing of experiences and a *biennial monitoring report (BMR)* that provides the evidence base to inform strategic assessment of the partnerships. The first report was published in May 2022 and the second is planned for 2024.
- *An intervention logic that focuses not only on market and systemic failures, but also on transformational failures* (e.g. shortage of skills or critical mass or cross-sectoral cooperation (Fig. 6.18)).

Source: selected from European Commission (2022)

Another form of Guidance of the search is the long-term R&D and production investment programmes and strategies adopted by leading multinational companies

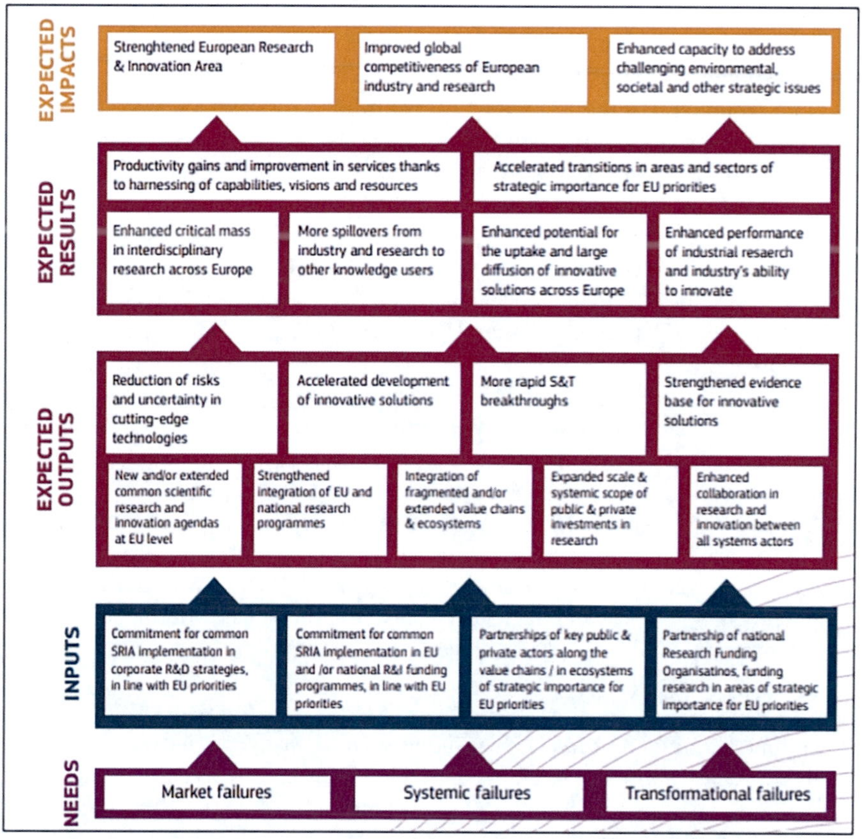

Fig. 6.18 Intervention logic of the European Partnerships programme. Source: European Commission (2022), p. 26

in various industrial sectors that support and complement the objectives of EU programmes such as Horizon Europe and the Horizon 2020 European Green Deal. Relevant examples include Volkswagen Group's 'Way to Zero' programme, Shell's Sky Scenario and Airbus *ZEROe Programme* (Box 6.6). They reflect the collaborative efforts between the public and private sectors aimed to drive innovation and sustainability in key areas that are essential for achieving climate goals and economic transformation.

Box 6.6 Long-Term R&D and Production Investment Programmes Adopted by Leading Multinational Companies That Support and Complement the EU R&I Programmes

- *Volkswagen Group's 'Way to Zero' programme*[35,36] focuses on achieving carbon neutrality by 2050, based on significant investments in electric vehicle technology, battery innovation and sustainable manufacturing processes. The company adopted an extensive package of decarbonisation measures supported by investments of €14 billion by 2025, to accelerate the sustainable production and use of electric cars and cut CO_2 emissions in Europe by an average of some 17 tons per vehicle by 2030—the equivalent of 40% less than in 2018. After offering customers the possibility to charge green electricity at home (Volkswagen Naturstrom) and on the road (e.g. at IONITY charging stations), the company is the first car maker to support the construction of new wind farms and solar plants in several regions of Europe by 2025, to expand large-scale provision of renewable energy. The solar plant built in Germany is the largest independent solar project in this country, with a total capacity of 170 million kilowatt hours each year and around 420,000 solar modules. Taking a step further towards sustainable production, the electricity for plants in Europe and North and South America will be switched to renewables by 2030.

  Sector: Automotive

- *Shell's Sky Scenario*[37] is a comprehensive strategic vision for achieving net-zero emissions by 2050 based on substantial R&D investment in renewable energy sources, carbon capture and storage (CCS) and development of hydrogen fuel technologies. The transformation of the global energy system is envisioned through coordinated efforts across various sectors and geographies to meet the goals of the Paris Agreement. For energy transition, the scenario envisages a significant shift from fossil fuels to renewable energy sources, with solar and wind energy providing up to 50% of global electricity by 2050. Natural gas is seen as a transitional fuel, helping to bridge the gap, while renewable technologies continue to scale up. Carbon capture and storage (CCS) technologies will be adopted to reduce atmospheric CO2 from both industrial processes and power generation. By 2070, it is projected that CCS will capture and store over

(continued)

[35] https://www.volkswagen.co.uk/en/electric-and-hybrid/living-electric/sustainability/way-to-zero.html

[36] https://www.volkswagen-newsroom.com/en/press-releases/way-to-zero-volkswagen-presents-roadmap-for-climate-neutral-mobility-7081

[37] https://www.fourleafdigital.shell.com/WebApps/SKY_assets/index.html

Box 6.6 (continued)

10 gigatonnes of CO_2 annually. The production and use of hydrogen are expected to increase significantly and play a key role in sectors that are hard to electrify, such as heavy industry and long-haul transportation. Such changes require continuous technological advancements in renewable energy, energy storage and grid management, as well as innovation in materials science and digital technologies. Scalability and affordability of emerging technologies are also key issues. These changes also require behavioural shifts and robust policy interventions to create jobs and retrain workers from declining sectors, increase energy efficiency and introduce carbon pricing mechanisms and policies promoting sustainable land use and deforestation prevention. These goals could only be achieved through close collaboration of governments and industries to create conducive regulatory environments and invest in necessary infrastructure but can encounter difficulties given varying economic priorities and capabilities.

Sector: Energy

- *Airbus ZEROe Programme*[38,39] develops the world's first zero-emission hydrogen-powered commercial aircraft by 2035 based on R&D on hydrogen propulsion and hybrid-electric technologies. By shifting to hydrogen-powered aircraft, Airbus seeks to eliminate CO_2 emissions from flights and reduce other pollutants such as nitrogen oxides (NO_x) and particulate matter. That can significantly reduce the aviation industry's carbon footprint, which accounts for a high portion of global greenhouse gas emissions. Airbus introduced three concept designs for the hydrogen-powered aircraft: a *Turbofan design* (for 120–200 passengers, a range of over 2000 nautical miles, for transcontinental flights), a *Turboprop design* (for up to100 passengers, a range of over 1000 nautical miles and shorter regional travel) and a *Blended-Wing Body design* (up to 200 passengers, unique configuration with a wide fuselage providing more space for hydrogen storage and distribution). The ZEROe initiative represents a potential paradigm shift in the aviation industry, pushing towards sustainable aviation and inspiring other manufacturers to explore zero-emission technologies. Successful implementation of the programme will necessitate changes in airport infrastructure, technological advancements in fuel cell technology and hydrogen combustion engines, updating of regulatory frameworks with new standards and certification processes and supply chains to accommodate the hydrogen-powered aircraft.

(continued)

[38] https://www.airbus.com/en/innovation/energy-transition/hydrogen/zeroe

[39] https://www.h2knowledgecentre.com/content/researchpaper3981

Box 6.6 (continued)
Sector: Aviation

- *Siemens' Smart Infrastructure Programme*[40,41] is a comprehensive initiative that focuses on creating intelligent, sustainable and resilient urban environments, along four main directions:

   (i) *Creating smart buildings* that use automation and data analytics to optimize energy consumption, enhance comfort and improve operational efficiency. Key solutions include Building Management Systems (BMS), smart thermostats, lighting controls and HVAC systems.
   (ii) *Advanced energy management solutions for electricity grids and renewable energy integration* to support the transition to more sustainable energy sources while ensuring grid stability and reliability (e.g. microgrids, smart metering and energy storage systems).
   (iii) *Digital solutions based on IoT, AI and cloud computing* to create smart ecosystems that adapt to changing conditions and optimize performance in real time (e.g. the Siemens Xcelerator platform uses digital twins and data analytics to simulate and manage complex infrastructures, with improved decision-making and operational efficiency).
   (iv) *Sustainability and resilience by reducing carbon footprints and promoting energy efficiency* through technologies that support renewable energy integration, energy-efficient building designs and sustainable urban planning. Resilience focuses on solutions to enhance the ability of infrastructures to withstand and recover from disruptions, whether they are natural disasters or cyberattacks.

Siemens' solutions contribute to urban development (smart cities) by providing interconnected systems for smart transportation systems, more efficient public services and public safety measures. The smart infrastructure solutions can save important costs for businesses and municipalities and create jobs in high-tech sectors. The programme also aims to significantly reduce greenhouse gas emissions, integrate renewable energy sources and enhance energy efficiency. Successful implementation of the initiative depends on the effective integration and interoperability of different technologies, ensuring data security and privacy and overcoming the obstacles raised by various regulatory provisions and market adoption challenges.

Sector: Infrastructure
Source: own elaboration

[40] https://www.siemens.com/global/en/company/about/businesses/smart-infrastructure.html

[41] https://assets.new.siemens.com/siemens/assets/api/uuid:3903ea1f-a289-446e-ba79-9215aeaa2e80/Smart-Infrastructure-Brochure-end-to-end-solution-47cmX33cm-Final-V5.pdf

6.7 Function: Creation of Legitimacy/Counteracting Resistance to Change

This function is represented to various degrees in virtually all the R&I projects analysed here but is explicitly addressed in one of the R&I project groups funded under the European Green Deal call of Horizon 2020, namely, 'Knowledge and citizens'[42] (16 projects). These projects aim to determine behavioural changes in large populations' lifestyles and expectations for facilitating the implementation of the European Green Deal. The projects use various data collection and monitoring instruments, emerging technologies (sensors, applications), citizen science and other participative approaches to change behaviour, create awareness and produce practical tools, policy recommendations and advocacy activities to address the Green Deal priorities. All the projects engage large communities of citizens and institutions (schools, universities, SMEs, local authorities, etc.) in several countries and regions.

These projects thus play a critical role in creating legitimacy and counteracting resistance to the green and digital transitions by demonstrating feasibility and benefits of green and digital innovations, reducing scepticism and building confidence among stakeholders, including industries, policymakers and the public. By engaging diverse stakeholders, they help to align interests, address concerns and co-create solutions that are more likely to gain acceptance and support. The projects also influence policymaking by providing evidence-based recommendations and demonstrating the need for regulatory adjustments that reduce resistance to change. Many projects include social innovation components that address potential negative impacts of transitions, such as job losses or social inequalities. By developing solutions that mitigate these concerns, they help to reduce opposition from affected communities. Finally, these projects have a strong educational and awareness-creating role, informing the public and stakeholders about the green and digital transitions and addressing concerns, thereby reducing resistance and fostering a smoother transition.

A selection of the most relevant projects with this focus are presented in Table 6.8.

[42] https://ec.europa.eu/research-and-innovation/en/strategy/strategy-2020-2024/environment-and-climate/european-green-deal/green-deal-projects-support/green-deal-projects-working-groups/knowledge-and-citizens

Table 6.8 R&I projects on 'Knowledge and citizens' contributing to Creation of legitimacy/counteracting resistance to change

Partnership	Purpose
ACCTING (AdvanCing behavioural Change Through an INclusive Green deal)	To understand the unequal impact of Green Deal policies on vulnerable groups, prevent inequalities and produce knowledge and innovations to advance behavioural change at individual and collective levels for an inclusive and equal European Green Deal
AURORA (Empowering a new generation of near zero-emission citizens)	To change citizens' behaviour and attitudes towards energy. Implemented as a demonstrator in five European countries where it aims to upgrade social communities (four university communities and one rural deprived area), to new civic consortia, to generate the first generations of Near Zero-Emission Citizens as ambassadors for sustainable energy behaviour
COMPAIR	To use Citizen Science for strengthening citizens' capacity to monitor, understand and change their environmental impact, both at a behavioural and policy level. A Citizen Science Lab runs experiments to supplement gaps in official air quality data to (a) co-create more effective social actions and (b) influence city policy.
ECF4CLIM (a European competence framework for a low-carbon economy and sustainability through education)	To develop, test and validate a European Competence Framework (ECF) for transformational change, which will empower the educational community to act against climate change and towards sustainable development. It applies a novel hybrid participatory approach, rooted in participatory action research and citizen science, to codesign the ECF in selected schools and universities
GreenSCENT (Smart Citizen Education for a Green Future)	To develop the GreenComp (European Sustainability Competence Framework) using both expert and researcher input and advice, citizen participation and stakeholder engagement. The framework is tested in different European regions, different educational levels (from primary schools to higher education—about 45 schools and universities across the EU). Pilots will implement collaborative learning, debates, research-based learning, inquiry-based learning and demonstrators, to include digital, physical and hybrid educational technologies.
REAL_DEAL (reshaping citizens' deliberation for the European Green Deal)	To stimulate a pan-European debate to reshape citizens' and stakeholders' active participation in deliberative democracy around the European Green Deal from a wide range of

(continued)

Table 6.8 (continued)

Partnership	Purpose
	disciplines (environmental rights and the law of public participation, ethics and responsible innovation, gender studies and ecofeminism, psychology, geography, urban planning and sustainability studies). It includes the EU's largest civil society networks advocating on the environment, climate, sustainable development, local democracy and the European movement, youth climate, social justice and women's organisations, small businesses, universities and research institutes and civil society
SOCIO-BEE (Wearables and droneS fOr CIty Socio-Environmental Observations and BEhavioral ChangE)	To use Citizen Science (CS) and emerging technologies (portable air quality sensors) for community engagement and social innovation to empower communities to adopt more sustainable behaviour and reduce air pollution
I-CHANGE	To provide citizens with practical tools and sensors, knowledge and solutions to reduce their own personal carbon and environmental footprint and to support climate adaptation and mitigation, triggering social innovation. Eight interactive Living Labs across Europe, Israel and Burkina Faso and a participatory platform—Environmental Impact Hub—will collect heterogeneous data and make it available to citizens, policymakers and other actors
PSLifestyle (Co-Creating a Positive and Sustainable Lifestyle tool with and for European Residents)	To enable citizens to actively create data while monitoring their lifestyle-induced climate impact and behaviour. The collected data will be used to create a digital application to co-research, codevelop and uptake everyday life solutions for climate change. It aims to engage a total of 4 million EU citizens

Source: selected from Green Deal Projects | Research and Innovation (europa.eu) (Knowledge and Citizens Working Group)

References

Dosi, G., Llerena, P., & Labini, M. S. (2006). The relationships between science, technologies and their industrial exploitation: An illustration through the myths and realities of the so-called 'European Paradox'. *Research Policy, 35*(10), 1450–1464. https://doi.org/10.1016/j.respol.2006.09.012

European Commission. (2020). *Horizon 2020 – European Green Deal call*. Directorate-General for Research and Innovation. Publications Office of the European Union. https://doi.org/10.2777/200559

European Commission. (2021). *The European Green Deal call for proposal in Horizon 2020*. Publications Office of the European Union. https://doi.org/10.2777/799749

European Commission. (2021a). COM(2021). *Annual single market report 2021. Updating the 2020 new industrial strategy: Building a stronger single market for Europe's recovery.* https://commission.europa.eu/system/files/2021-05/swd-annual-single-market-report-2021_en.pdf

European Commission. (2021b). *The European Green Deal call for proposal in Horizon 2020.* Directorate-General for Research and Innovation, Publications Office of the European Union. https://doi.org/10.2777/799749

European Commission. (2022). *Performance of European partnerships – Biennial monitoring report 2022 on partnerships in Horizon Europe.* Directorate-General for Research and Innovation. Publications Office of the European Union. https://doi.org/10.2777/144363

European Commission. (2022a). *European partnerships contributing to the green transition.* Directorate-General for Research and Innovation. Publications Office of the European Union. https://doi.org/10.2777/568910

European Commission. (2022b). *European partnerships for the digital and industrial transition.* Directorate-General for Research and Innovation. Publications Office of the European Union. https://doi.org/10.2777/89438

European Commission. (2022c). SWD(2022) 40 final PART ½. *Annual single market report 2022.* https://data.consilium.europa.eu/doc/document/ST-6499-2022-INIT/en/pdf

European Commission. (2023). *Monitoring European industrial ecosystems conceptual, monitoring and indicator framework.* https://monitor-industrial-ecosystems.ec.europa.eu/sites/default/files/2023-12/EMI%20Methodological%20Report.pdf

European Commission. (2023a). SWD(2023) 26 final PART 1/5. *2023 Annual Single Market Report: Single Market at 30.* https://single-market-economy.ec.europa.eu/system/files/2023-01/ASMR 2023.pdf.

Chapter 7
Towards Single Market 2.0: The Innovation Road

Abstract Applying the framework of the seven functions of an innovation system to assess the impact of the European Green Deal on the Single Market's industrial ecosystems reveals substantial transformations. These changes are fuelled by the R&I projects funded under selected calls of Horizon 2020 and Horizon Europe and pave the way to a 'Single Market 2.0'. The technologies developed in this context offer a promising outlook for the future of the Single Market but, with few exceptions, have low to medium market readiness levels. A thorough evaluation of their impact will necessitate additional time, data and research. The long-term success of these technological developments also hinges on the capacity to overcome high implementation costs, structural disparities among the Member States, social acceptance and the ability to build stronger synergies between industrial, competitiveness and innovation policies.

Applying the analytical framework of the seven functions of an innovation system to the Single Market and its industrial ecosystems, we identified significant transformations driven by the R&I projects financed through selected calls of Horizon 2020 and Horizon Europe aligned with the European Green Deal objectives:

- *The Knowledge development function* has showcased various activities focused on knowledge creation, education, training and skills enhancement for both industry and non-industry professionals in numerous knowledge and technology areas. These activities generate substantial knowledge outcomes and advance the industrial ecosystems' knowledge and technology base, integrating sustainability initiatives across sectors and institutions.
- *The Knowledge diffusion/exchange through networks function* has shown the formation of large and dense consortia and networks of Quadruple Helix stakeholders (universities, research and technology centres, SMEs and large companies, clusters, government authorities and other public bodies, civil society, non-governmental organisations, etc.) around the R&I projects focused on the green and digital transitions. The consortia and networks span several geographies (regional, national and international, involving EU countries as well as associated and third countries) and engage diverse communities of public and

M. Ranga, *Single Market 2.0*, Contributions to Economics,
https://doi.org/10.1007/978-3-031-83220-8_7

private organisations both across Europe and beyond. They foster collaboration across various types of networks (research, innovation, business, industrial, technological, cultural) contributing to a broad territorial spread of the EU's knowledge, technology, and industrial capabilities. These consortia and networks generated multiple secondary projects, technical workshops, stakeholder fora, open events, open calls, conferences, exchanges, publications, etc. Considering their various geographic locations across the EU, these consortia and networks reflect strategic concentrations of the EU's knowledge, technology and industrial assets within single nations or regions or in broad interregional or transnational formats. Notably, the 11 Joint Undertakings (JUs) that comprise large EU consortia and networks, have enabled high levels of public and private investment for their research, technological development and demonstration programmes.

- *The Market formation and Entrepreneurial activity functions*, taken together here, considering the close connections between them, demonstrate that the R&I projects funded by the European Green Deal under Horizon 2020 and Horizon Europe contribute to market formation by enabling comprehensive testing, demonstration and scaling of innovative technologies through a variety of living labs, trials and pilots, city hubs, large-scale demonstrators, etc. These activities help create niche markets, foster demand for new products and support the development of environmental standards. They also facilitate data sharing and connect businesses with global markets, promoting European competitiveness. Many projects develop new or disruptive technologies in Europe and stimulate their integration across critical sectors and strategic industries, supporting the EU's competitiveness and technical sovereignty. At the same time, these projects enhance entrepreneurship by providing platforms for collaboration among start-ups, SMEs and research institutions, helping them turn innovative ideas into marketable products. This is especially critical in sectors with strict regulatory requirements, such as healthcare and aviation, aiding start-ups in market entry and growth through knowledge transfer, business incubation and networking opportunities. These efforts address the 'European paradox', which highlights Europe's challenge in translating scientific advances into marketable innovations.
- *The Resource mobilisation function* has highlighted the large amounts of public and private investments for the green and digital transitions mobilised by the R&I projects from the EU Member States and Associated Countries, national budgets and the private sector and their multi-annual allocation.
- *The Guidance of the search function*, considered here as a complex set of governance, policymaking and policy-influencing activities that determine specific industry trends, technologies, standards and certification processes, has revealed different roles played by several partners. The European Commission exerts a crucial role through the design and management of funding programmes, through the novel elements introduced in eligibility rules, funding allocation or evaluation. Public and private partners in the Quadruple Helix consortia mentioned above also contribute to this function by shaping industry trends, influencing EU or national policies and accelerating the adoption of new regulations and

standards. Many major multinational companies, such as Volkswagen, Shell and Airbus, aligned their long-term R&D and investment strategies with the EU objectives. All these dynamics reflect a variety of collaborative efforts between the public and private sectors aimed to drive innovation and sustainability in areas that are essential for climate goals and economic transformation.

- *The Creation of legitimacy/Counteracting resistance to change function* is represented in various degrees in virtually all R&I projects analysed but is distinctly visible in the 'Knowledge and Citizens' project group funded under the Horizon 2020 European Green Deal call (16 projects). These projects explicitly aim to induce behavioural changes in society, raise awareness, influence behaviour and provide practical tools and policy recommendations to support the European Green Deal's implementation, using data collection tools, emerging technologies, citizen science and participatory approaches. Engaging diverse stakeholders, these projects build legitimacy and work towards reducing resistance to the green and digital transitions and addressing concerns, including those related to social impacts such as job losses.

The R&I projects examined in our analysis give a promising outlook for the Single Market in the coming years, paving the way to a 'Single Market 2.0'. However, the effectiveness of these projects in reaching the set objectives is still to be proven. Since many of the projects are still running, a full and accurate assessment of their impact requires more time, data and research efforts, as well as a careful consideration of other effects at regional, country and global level, as well as at sectoral and firm level. Some relevant answers can be obtained from a few programme evaluation reports currently available. For example, the recent ex-post evaluation of Horizon 2020 (European Commission, 2024) provides comprehensive assessments of the overall programme that apply also to the R&I projects in our sample, acknowledging the inherent difficulties of the evaluation: *'evaluating R&I activities is challenging because of the nature of knowledge generation and its diffusion process. It takes time for R&I activities to produce results, outcomes, and impacts because of the importance of trial and errors, with an inherent need for risk taking and failures. The question of attribution of the effects observed is another challenge as scientific progress builds on knowledge that cumulates over decades and spreads unexpectedly in multiple domains and applications'* (Section 1 Introduction).

The evaluation highlights that the market readiness levels of the new technologies promoted by the Horizon 2020 projects are predominantly low. Based on the low number of patent applications reported by project participants, the evaluation finds that most technologies are at a low to medium maturity level and not yet ready for patenting, with a few exceptions in the areas of Internet of Things, advanced computing and advanced materials that had a slightly higher proportion of market-ready innovations. The Innovation Radar confirmed this observation, showing that although the programme has funded potentially ground-breaking technological innovations, over half of all innovations recorded are in an 'Exploring' stage (53%) and only 17% are considered ready for market introduction.

The evaluation also remarks the extensive investments in artificial intelligence, quantum computing and clean energy technologies, including hydrogen fuels and clean aviation, but comparatively less funding for climate-related R&I (only 32%, just below the promised 35% of its EUR 75.6 billion investment). The time span for observable effects needs to be considered as well, as many projects supported by the programme yield effects in the medium to long term, such as health projects on rare diseases and therapies and personalised medicine and projects with societal impact in terms of security and environment. The evaluation also remarks the difficulty in measuring the real-world impact of these achievements, caused not only by the long-term span for observing impact but also by the narrow scope and weaknesses of the monitoring indicators used by Horizon 2020.

The successful impact of the green and digital technologies supported by the R&I projects analysed here also needs to consider several other factors:

- *The growth potential of these technologies in various countries and regions, especially in rural communities and less developed regions.* This depends significantly on the specific economic and industrial structure conditions, and in many cases, it is also a matter of social acceptance. The deployment of large-scale renewable energy projects, such as wind farms and solar power plants, has often been met with resistance due to concerns related to deforestation, noise pollution, visual impact, potential disruption of local ecosystems, loss of biodiversity and valuable habitat for plants and animals or the capacity of the grid infrastructure to handle the variability of renewable energy sources. This is the case in Spain, for example, which has seen a massive increase in renewable energy projects especially in the southern countryside. As the government intends to produce at least 74% of its electricity from renewable energy by 2030, the country has seen increasingly frequent protests and campaigns against these projects from angry farmers—some of whom have been expropriated—and even from some ecologists (Morris et al., 2023; Rodríguez-Segura et al., 2023). In many cases, these projects have been implemented in low-cost marginal soils of high ecological value, such as extensive cereal farmlands and wild mountain ranges that provide unique habitats for some declining species, and fail to provide an in-depth assessment of cumulative and synergistic environmental impacts (Serrano et al., 2020). In Germany, the deployment of wind turbines has been delayed or scaled back due to legal challenges and fierce resistance from the locals, who fear health risks, destruction of forests or ruining the view of cultural sites (Wehrmann, 2019; Pladson, 2023).

Other factors at play, especially in rural areas, are the high costs and low population density, which raised challenges to the deployment of high-speed Internet, leading to slower adoption of digital technologies that are crucial for modern agriculture, education and small businesses. In France, 5G has helped narrow the urban-rural gap, with rural areas now experiencing better connectivity than before, although the gap remains significant (Khatri, 2024). In Italy, rural areas are behind urban centres in terms of broadband and 5G deployment, as the high costs of infrastructure development in sparsely populated regions make it less attractive for telecom companies to invest heavily (Wyrzykowski, 2022). High cost and low population density in rural areas have also hindered the adoption of electric vehicles and construction of charging infrastructure in countries like Ireland, Malta and Cyprus, which have low recharging power per vehicle, despite a significant potential (European Alternative Fuels Observatory, 2024).

- *The uneven EU investment flows among the industrial ecosystems, which risk creating new development disparities within the Single Market as a whole.* As discussed in Chap. 6, the uneven concentrations of EU R&I funding (high in some ecosystems, such as Energy-Renewables and Energy-Intensive industries, Digital and Electronics, Agri-Food and Health, and low in other ecosystems, such as Textiles, Cultural and Creative Industries, Construction, and Tourism), can affect the capacity of the less funded ecosystems to implement green and digital technologies in the longer run. The experience of S3 implementation can be useful lesson in this respect, as it has shown that the more developed regions with already strong innovation, technology and industrial potential are likely to be further strengthened, while the less developed or transition regions that have various deficits in innovation, technology industrial potential and institutional capacity will have even more difficulty to catch up.
- *Stronger synergies between industrial, competition, innovation and regional development policies, as well as the provision of more data and evidence to document their mutual influences.* While synergies between innovation policy and regional development/cohesion policy have been documented in a few EC reports and scholarly papers (e.g. European Commission, 2022; Corpakis, 2020), the relations between competition, industrial and innovation policies have been much less explored. The close connections between industrial and innovation policies are clearly articulated in a 2015 UNCTAD Report: 'the notion of sustainable industrialization is multi-faceted: it is not solely limited to environmental sustainability, but refers to efforts that are technology-led, productivity enhancing and poverty-reducing. It is based on the understanding that no industrial policy is complete without an accompanying innovation policy. Both are essential and complementary to shaping developmental outcomes and creating prosperity for all' (UNCATD, 2015, page iii). Similar conclusions come also from a recent OECD report that investigates the ways in which competition drives innovation and how innovation, in turn, can shape competition and drive higher welfare and economic growth (OECD, 2023). However, the relationship between these policy areas in the context of the EU and the Single Market, especially considering the new demands and challenges posed by the European Green Deal, the twin transition, sustainable development and the global economic downturn, has not received sufficient attention.

The analysis of the Single Market through the innovation system lens offers valuable insights that are not sufficiently captured by the existing indicators. The activities taking place within each of the seven functions of the Single Market's industrial ecosystems reveal not only a process of technological development and learning in strategic sectors but also the development of technological infrastructures, networks and skills, the emergence of new markets and a societal transformation involving Quadruple Helix stakeholders from various geographies, that are essential for fostering the Single Market's sustainable competitiveness. In this context, the role attributed to research and innovation in the recent Communication *Long-term competitiveness of the EU: looking beyond 2030* (European Commission, 2023) as one of the nine 'mutually reinforcing drivers' of Single Market's sustainable competitiveness does not fully clarify how these mutually reinforcing effects between innovation and sustainable competitiveness take place.

To successfully transform the Single Market's industrial ecosystems, the synergies between industrial, competitiveness and innovation policy incentives and instruments must be better understood and more clearly articulated. This requires coordinated policy implementation not only within the European Commission bodies responsible for these areas but also at the national level across EU Member States, in terms of policies, incentives, funding mechanisms and agency mandates, which would further impact stakeholders such as firms and knowledge institutions. In the EU's rapidly evolving technological landscape, effective exploitation of synergies between industrial, competitiveness and innovation policies is crucial. It can become the 'North Star' guiding the Single Market's journey on its road to the future: the Innovation Road.

References

Corpakis, D. (2020). Powering synergies between innovation policy and regional development frameworks: The case of smart specialisation. In A. Abu-Tair, A. Lahrech, K. Al Marri, & B. Abu-Hijleh (Eds.), *Proceedings of the II international triple helix summit*. THS 2018 (Lecture notes in civil engineering) (Vol. 43). Springer. https://doi.org/10.1007/978-3-030-23898-8_8

European Alternative Fuels Observatory. (2024, May 10). *EAFO analysis: Trends in EV charging infrastructure across Europe*. https://alternative-fuels-observatory.ec.europa.eu/general-information/news/eafo-analysis-trends-ev-charging-infrastructure-across-europe

European Commission. (2022). *Synergies between ERDF programmes and Horizon Europe*. https://research-and-innovation.ec.europa.eu/document/download/6c6230d0-de1a-4280-9289-67234d8e4e94_en?filename=c_2022_4747_1_en_annex.pdf

European Commission. (2023). COM(2023) 168 final. *Long-term competitiveness of the EU: Looking beyond 2030*. https://commission.europa.eu/system/files/2023-03/Communication_Long-term-competitiveness.pdf

European Commission. (2024). SWD(2024) 29 final. *Ex-post evaluation of Horizon 2020, the EU framework programme for research and innovation*. https://eur-lex.europa.eu/legal-content/EN/TXT/?uri=SWD%3A2024%3A29%3AFIN&qid=1706528145182

Khatri, H. (2024, May 7). *France's urban-rural mobile experience gap has narrowed with 5G*. Open Signal. https://www.opensignal.com/2024/05/07/frances-urban-rural-mobile-experience-gap-has-narrowed-with-5g

Morris, S., Exposito, A. & Schmitt, C. (2023, June 16). Spanish farmers in battle against giant solar parks. Focus. https://www.france24.com/en/tv-shows/focus/20230616-spanish-farmers-in-battle-against-giant-solar-parks

OECD. (2023). *Competition and innovation: A theoretical perspective.* OECD Competition Policy Roundtable Background Note. https://www.oecd.org/daf/competition/competition-and-innovation-a-theoretical-perspective-2023.pdf

Pladson, K. (2023, February 17). Germany's wind energy: Conservationists fear for forests. Deutsche Welle. https://www.dw.com/en/germanys-wind-energy-conservationists-fear-for-forests/a-64731998

Rodríguez-Segura, F. J., Osorio-Aravena, J. C., Frolova, M., Terrados-Cepeda, J., & Muñoz-Cerón, E. (2023). Social acceptance of renewable energy development in southern Spain: Exploring tendencies, locations, criteria and situations. *Energy Policy, 173*, 113356. https://doi.org/10.1016/j.enpol.2022.113356

Serrano, D., Margalida, A., Perz-Garcia, J. M., et al. (2020). Renewables in Spain threaten biodiversity. *Science, 370*(6522), 1282–1283. https://doi.org/10.1126/science.abf650

UNCATD. (2015). *Fostering innovation policies for industrial development. Overview.* https://unctad.org/system/files/official-document/tir2015overview_en.pdf

Wehrmann, B. (2019, March 27). *Limits to growth: Resistance against wind power in Germany.* Clean Energy Wire. https://www.cleanenergywire.org/factsheets/fighting-windmills-when-growth-hits-resistance

Wyrzykowski, R. (2022, August 30). *The rural urban divide widens with 5G rollouts in Italy*. Open Signal. https://www.opensignal.com/2022/08/30/the-rural-urban-divide-widens-with-5g-rollouts-in-italy

The manufacturer's authorised representative in the EU is Springer Nature Customer Service Centre GmbH, Europaplatz 3, 69115 Heidelberg, Germany. If you have any concerns regarding our products, please contact ProductSafety@springernature.com

Printed and bound by CPI Group (UK) Ltd, Croydon, CR0 4YY
06/10/2026
02225878-0004